Life's Journey

by

David J. Dove

Copyright

Acknowledgements

To all my wonderful patients from whose courage and determination in facing their own demons I learned humility, some of the meaning of life and how to overcome its' difficulties; to Angus McLeod and others for their inspiration and friendship through the hard times; for Angie Summers who allowed me to believe; to Nigel Sprent for his years of steady guidance and balancing views; to Vanessa for her love and encouragement and to all those who may have trespassed against me in life and thereby made me stronger – Thank You!

Introduction.

For nearly twenty years I have been practising as a Psychotherapist in England and what follows is no more than a summary of that which I have learned about life from the many wonderful people who entrusted me with their emotional and mental wellbeing during that time. We worked together to overcome issues and concerns that they felt were in some way limiting their enjoyment of life or preventing them reaching their full potential and, whilst doing so, I feel that I learned at least as much from them as they, hopefully, learned from me.

Almost the only surprise to me in all that time was not the variety of psychological and emotional conditions that were brought to me but the similarity of their cases in terms of what was required to help the client overcome their perceived limitations and become more content with themselves as a whole person, able to enjoy life on their own terms. I concluded that the majority were suffering not from any of the complex underlying conditions so clearly laid out and labelled within so many erudite text books, but rather a lack of understanding of life itself, and how it worked, which gave rise to neuroses, anxiety and stress.

Filled with misperceptions and self-limiting beliefs created by the world that they had grown up in, they appeared to be imprisoned in a life that they did not deserve, were not enjoying but from which they could find no escape, indeed, many felt that there could be no such thing as escape, that this was their fate and that was it.

Female clients in particular were all too often accepting of their assigned role as drudges, slaves, objects of scorn/use, targets of abuse or mere playthings. Willing, loving servant of their partner, their parents, their children, their friends and colleagues and anyone else who cared to make a demand on them, they all to often had no time to, or for, themselves, failing to see that they too were an individual with needs and were an equal to everyone else, not only in their own world but in THE world. These people in particular inspired me to try to reveal to them an alternative side of life through therapy such that they were able to restore their self esteem and sense of self worth and value themselves as individuals, equal to all, living a more meaningful life according to their own values, not those of others.

We seem to teach our children the rules of life but not how to actually live life. As a consequence, as individuals we often fail to reach our full potential, spending, as we do, far too much time battling with life instead of living it to the full. Too much of our time is lost in conforming and fitting in, "doing the right thing" according to others' rules and ideas of what is right, being concerned about what others may think about us instead of being ourself and allowing our natural talents to shine through, and to be truly content with who we are.

This book therefore is about passing on that distilled understanding in order that you may take from it that which you recognise as being of use to yourself. It is not intended as a template for life, there are already far too many of those, nor is it a rule book, quite the reverse.

Dip in and out at will; some of it may ring a bell with you, some of it may possibly seem trite or perhaps even too difficult at the moment, that's OK, just take what you need, when you need it because what you need from it will change with time as you grow and develop as a person. Feel free to disagree, reject or hold totally opposing views, as long as you hold your views to be your own truth, arrived at by thoughtful consideration and personal experience and not through the imposition of others, then so it is. This is only meant to challenge entrenched self-limiting thoughts, to grow emergent beliefs in self and explain what might be possible if we understand better why life is the way it appears to be.

Life is a journey; we don't remember the beginning and we try to ignore the end usually until it is too late and so all that we can do is enjoy the bit in-between – our life. Your own life is unique and precious and you are just as important and valuable as any other person on this planet, it's just difficult to remember that sometimes when the world seems to be against us and others try to make us believe quite differently.

The world is not really against us, the world is strictly neutral; the universe doesn't care if we live or die or whether we are rich or poor or happy or sad – it is just our own personal interpretation of events that leads us to believe otherwise and thereby limits our enjoyment of daily life.

So, the first lesson is – if the neutral universe really doesn't mind how we are then we can choose to be a happy person rather than a sad person and we can choose to be whatever we want to be, all we have to do is lose, or change, our self limiting beliefs and habits to become our new self.

Easy? No, not really, but not that difficult either, it just takes enough courage to be who you really are already and to live your own life, not someone else's and to stop thinking (worrying) so much, stop "what-if'ing" or "if-only"ing and just appreciate what you have and who you really are underneath all the worldly image and "front" that we all feel we have to protect ourselves with. As soon as we stop listening to our busy, busy mind and listen instead to our quiet, instinctive knowledge then we can become who we really are and all that we can possibly be. In other words, to realise our full potential. Lose your mind and come to your senses is a common saying that has a lot of truth within it.

Whose life are you actually living at the moment? You may feel that that is a foolish question as we can only experience one life, our own and no-one else's. What I mean is that by whose rules, needs and expectations are you living your life – your own that you have developed over time and personal experience and belief or someone else's that heave been instilled in you?

You will be surprised to learn that it is probably not your own entirely, if at all. The next chapter will explain why I say that before we move onto helping you change into who you really are, then we will look at how to become the person that you can really be to make yourself truly happy in life. It's your life, no one else's and so only you can make the necessary changes to become the person that you truly wish to be, it's your responsibility to be happy, no one else's. Want to be happy with yourself?

Have a great journey!

Chapter 1 - We are where we are.

We spend a lot of our life thinking "if only" thoughts such as "if only I were rich, if only I lived in another country, if only I was taller/ shorter / whiter/ browner/ married/ single/ thinner/ blond/ dark-haired" etc etc. While such thoughts can be comforting or discomforting they will not actually achieve the change that we need to enable us to enjoy our life to the full, they just add to our worry-heap, and this worry-heap needs constant maintenance, going round and round in our heads on an hour by hour, day by day basis which can be extremely wearing, draining and exhausting both mentally and emotionally. There are no excuses or simple answers – we are where we are – the only question is, what are we going to do about it?

Acceptance.

Not a big word but a mighty big concept to get our head around and one that is often misunderstood. Acceptance in this sense does not mean accepting that something is right, or just, or fair; it may not be, it means simply accepting that it is so. It is what it is, I am where I am, I may not like it or have wished it or planned to be here, but I am, so I have to work with that fact and until I do so nothing will change for the better.

It might not be right, or fair, or just that we are there, but we are. No amount of "life's not fair" or "it's not my fault" thinking, or complaining and moaning to others will change a thing, only action on our own part now will change anything for the better.

Afraid to change? Remember, if you keep doing what you have always done, you will keep getting the result that you have always got. To paraphrase Einstein, to keep doing the same thing while expecting a different result is madness. Lesson one, if you want to change anything about your life only you can do it. Lesson two. If you can't be bothered to change aspects of your life that you unhappy about, but are within your control, stop complaining about it. The world is full of people who merely complain but don't take action. Make up your mind which you wish to be.

The following chapters will give you some ways of accepting and making changes in a measured and practical way that do not appear daunting and will encourage you to continue with the changes that you want to make in your life.

For now, just accept that yes, life is not fair (but then, who said it was?) and you can then begin to change the "what is" for what you would like it to be. I shall return to this theme later because many of us do get hung up on this totally ridiculous fallacy that life should somehow be fair, and we lose time and expend great effort in complaining about it while standing still in life instead of getting on with it. Life, in fact, is neither fair nor unfair, it just is. It is only our own interpretation that we put on things that makes it appear to be unfair – change your mind (interpretation) to change your luck (life).

Note the emphasis on the "you" in "..you can then begin to change the "what is..." above, no one else can or will change it for you, no one else has the need or the responsibility for changing it. It's your life and only your life, no one else's and the responsibility is entirely yours now.

It was different when you were a child, you were the subject of control by others but now that you are grown up that can no longer be an excuse; if what you have got doesn't suit – change it! I repeat the old saying that "If you keep doing what you have always done you will keep getting what you have always got". Change it or stay where and as you are, it's your **choice** – another big concept to accept.

Choice.

Effectively, you are in a prison, a mental/emotional/behavioural prison created by all those care givers who, hopefully with the best of intentions, were responsible for your upbringing as a child and a young adult. Parents, family relations, other adults, authority figures such as teachers, guardians and later perhaps police and yes, even the much loved traffic wardens who tell you the rules of society and remind you more forcefully, and perhaps punitively, if you break them. Note that we are only told the rules of the society in which we grow up (and are punished for breaking them), not the rules of life! How useful would that be if we were taught those and rewarded for keeping them instead of being punished for breaking them? What follows are some of the rules of life and the rewards for keeping them that can lead to a more relaxed, enjoyable life.

Whilst growing up we are subject to many and varied influences from all directions, some good, some bad. It is how we react to those influences that will determine who we will be as an adult. Even the social status of our parents and their financial standing, where we were brought up and the manner of doing so all impacts our belief systems in ourselves as adults. We may feel better than him or her or inadequate by comparison, we may feel embarrassed about our past or conscious that we don't speak with the correct accent and so on and on we go, pulling ourselves down. Stop it! If you spend this moment either regretting the past or worrying about the future all that you do is lose this moment, which you could be using to change your life for the better.

All that happened to us in the past couldn't be helped and can't be changed now, it's the past. Now is the present and while we can't change the past we can change the way we feel about it and the way that we allow it to influence our feelings about ourselves today.

Until now we were in that mental/emotional prison created by others and we had no choice because we weren't aware of it. Now – right now, through awareness, we have choice. We are not victims anymore. We can change anything about ourselves that we choose to. We have choice over every aspect of our lives every waking second of our life. The alternative to making those choices is to make excuses. Which are you doing? From the end of this sentence you are now aware of these facts and as a result you now have no choice but to exercise choice. Choosing to do nothing is still a choice we may make. What are you going to choose to do about your life? Something or nothing? If nothing, put this book down and go back to playing games. If your choice is to do something, read on and learn about more positive choices that you can easily make.

Starter Pack.

The only thing that all those people who influenced our young lives meant to give us, with the best of intentions, was a starter-pack for life. A starter pack of ethics, morals, beliefs, standards and behaviours which would have been based upon their own, not your, beliefs and experiences. Note that that is a starter-pack for life not a for-life pack for starters. It was only meant to provide us with guidance to keep us safe and out of trouble and to be acceptable to society around us until such time as we could think for ourselves – **at which point we were supposed to modify that early guidance to more closely reflect our own individual adult experience, develop our own personality, making our own decisions and substituting elements of the starter pack with our own self-created beliefs!**

But no one told us that bit and so typically we carry around with us a lot of instructions, rules, expectations and beliefs that, while they were appropriate to start with as a child, they may no longer be appropriate for us as a thinking, adult individual. They were someone else's rules, not our own. As a result we feel stressed by other people's expectations and their opinions of us, limited by rules that no longer apply to us and self limiting beliefs that we should have outgrown and could leave behind if we were only aware of their continued presence. We can only **accept** that and **choose** to change it.

Fear.

There are many reasons why we may choose not to change our life but key among them will be our fear of life in general and aspects of it in particular, unique to each of us. Again we are prisoners, this time of our fears. Fear of the new for example, fear of change, fear of choice, fear of consequences, fear of up-setting or offending others; on and on it goes, excuse after excuse, all seemingly "valid" reasons not to change our unhappiness for something better. How weird is that?

When I ask people "Why are you choosing to be so unhappy?" they normally put up a stout defence along the lines of "I am not choosing" (wrong), "I don't have a choice" (wrong), or "it's not my decision" (wrong), or "My parents would never speak to me again" (So?). The only honest answer that I ever heard was along the lines of "I could make that choice/change but the con-sequences would be worse than the present situation and so I choose not to change things – **at the moment**". Perfectly valid answer, the individual accepted the situation, took responsibility for their choice and was happy to live with it – for now! But - they might choose to make a different decision if any of the criteria change, perhaps tomorrow? Nothing is forever. I am where I am – at the moment. Tomorrow might bring the change in circumstance that will enable me to make a different decision and change my life in some small way for the better and so I keep it under review with a positive mindset looking for the opportunity to change something for the better.

We often fear failure, fear to try anything new lest we fail. We are trapped, imprisoned by fear and so we continue in our unhappy state, afraid to seek happiness because we cannot see beyond the prison fence in our mind. Another old saying has it that there is nothing to fear but fear itself and I have demonstrated the truth of this countless times to my own satisfaction in the opening up of positive choices or alternatives.

One mantra that I have already expressed and that I asked my patients to accept and practise was that "If you waste this moment either regretting the past or fearing the future then all that you do is waste this moment which could be used for positive change". Our life is short and, I suggest, is not to be wasted staring at it like a rabbit in the headlights, afraid to move or change or accomplish anything other than immobility. That will come soon enough at the end of our life without wasting this present time imitating it. Now is the time for action and doing things, for living life while we still have the strength, energy and the will to do so, to enjoy life to the full. Another old saying is that today we are creating tomorrow's memories. What sort of memory will you be creating today?

One type of fear that imprisons us is that of existential fear, of which we hear very little, but is so fundamental that it is common to everyone, yes, everyone (and yes, that means you as well), whether they are aware of it or not. I would like to focus on one aspect of this group of fears and I have already alluded to it – the fear of responsibility for our own lives.

This stems from an associated fear, that of loneness. Note, loneness not loneliness, that's different. Loneness is the knowledge within us that each of us is here on earth on our own. We may choose to surround ourselves with partners, family, friends, colleagues and associates, join clubs of like-minded people etc.but essentially, we are alone in the world and as such are solely responsible for our own life.

From this fundamental fear springs the dislike of taking responsibility for making decisions about our life on our own, we like to ask other peoples opinions, act in concert with others, to be a part of a known group like family or club or team. Change therefore requires decisions, which we alone are responsible for, and that reminds us at a very visceral level of the unpleasant truth and presence of loneliness. When we continually seek others opinions about the detail of our life it makes us dependent upon their views not our own and others, no matter how close to us or how well meaning they may be, always have their own agenda when providing opinions, agendas which aren't necessarily the same as our own. This seeking of opinion then also traps us into seeking other's approval by acting on their advice, for not to do so risks offending them, we might think, and so we follow their path, not our own.

Results.

The result is that we become dependent upon the goodwill and good opinions of others, we thereby become "other" referent rather than "self" referent and this undermines our self esteem and self worth. We find it difficult to follow an agenda which is best for us in case we upset or offend others. We "fit in" with other's requirements or opinions and then may become resentful about doing so as we then don't feel free to be ourselves. This resentment, unless openly expressed and resolved, remains within us as stress or anxiety which only serves as a negative influence upon our day to day thoughts, feelings and actions.

But we often don't express that resentment directly, or don't refuse to comply because, again, it might offend others and so we keep it in and experience it as general unhappiness or something worse, stress related illness for example. The choice, or question therefore is, to get ill or get out! Which is it to be?

Are you really living your life or just passing time on earth? Do you actually _feel_ alive? Are you excited about tomorrow? Some people expect life to be one long pleasure ride, it rarely is, while others expect it to be one long unending trail of misery, again, it rarely is. The old saying of "life is what you make it" has a grain of truth in it and a positive attitude and realistic expectations (of which more later) can lessen the dips and enhance smaller pleasures such that life is at least bearable with some pleasurable anticipation to keep us going.

If you enjoy convoluted logic try this: Life is difficult, but if you accept that it is (difficult) then it ceases to be (difficult) and just is. It is what it is. What that means is that life being difficult is the norm, not the exception, and the sooner that we learn to get rid of false expectations and learn to deal on a daily basis with everyday realities or difficulties the happier we will be.

Life is difficult, we know that so why do we expect it to be anything else, that way lies disappointment, frustration and unhappiness. If we just accept that it is difficult and deal with it the way it is and not the way we would like it to be then it ceases to be difficult because now that difficulty is normal – it is what it is – difficult is the new black! – and because we expect it to be so we can then accept the level of difficulty (normality) and just get on with it, no surprises or disappointments, no unhappiness because we expect it to be this way. Positive thinking in action!

Finally, who are you really and why aren't you being you? You can choose to remain as you are or you can choose to change and enjoy life more. It's your choice, no one else's. It's your life. Not to decide is a decision in itself, a decision to stay the same. If you are happy with that, excellent, I wish you every joy of your life. If you decide to change, excellent, I wish you every joy of your new life.

Dare to be yourself, dare to **escape** from the self imposed prison. The following chapter provides some insights as to how that might be possible.

Chapter 2 - Escape from what is.

To escape from our mental/emotional prison we need to understand a few of the things that have been imposed on us over the years by others, things that have led to us being where we are, both mentally and emotionally. By "things" I mean beliefs, understandings, "truths", other people's wishes, needs, imperatives, duties and all the hundred and one things that we think and believe we know about life and ourselves, but which, in truth, are just constructs of our mind and are as flimsy as tissue paper in a gale, to be blown away by the lightest breath of new thinking.

A modern phenomenon is the "selfie", a moment in time captured on a phone camera, usually of ourself in a momentarily interesting circumstance, the camera being pointed such that we are in the picture as well as the interesting background. This records that we were there when "it" happened. In truth, that is the last thing that it recorded. Because we were so busy creating and framing the picture we weren't actually "there" at all, our attention was not on the circumstance but on the recording of it. And so we miss true engagement with the moment. Classically we do this at a music festival and instead of listening to the music played live on spectacularly expensive equipment we doom ourselves to re-create it in a tinny sound on a tiny speaker in a 'phone. We may have been there physically but we weren't present, in the moment, experiencing it to the full. We talk more of this later in Mindfulness.

I choose this as a metaphor for what we do with life; standing by, watching it go past, re-living it later in our heads usually in an "if only" manner. We miss the richness of direct experience by being an observer of life, never living it to the full. Life happens in the moment, not in retrospect or on television and this moment, right now, is all that we have and, as previously mentioned, if we spend this moment either regretting the past or fearing the future all that we do is lose this moment. This moment will never come again; or this one, or this one. That is how we allow our life to drift past, moment by moment. Moments become hours, become days, become years and so our life passes us by. One old cliché that bears repeating is that today we are creating tomorrow's memories. What great memories will you be creating today?

The alternative is to plan a new way of life, to be present every moment, being pro-active, not reactive, in dealing with life, taking it on head-on, experiencing both the good and the bad for what it is, just life, and accepting it. To stop worrying about what MIGHT happen or DID happen and experience instead what IS happening.

All too often we create inaction by endlessly "what-iff"ing every circumstance that arises of any importance. What if it goes wrong? What if the neighbours see me doing that? What if "they" don't do what they say they will do? While some of that is necessary and prudent there comes a point at which it is counter productive and inhibits action. While we should be prudent about planning our life, for example with pensions, just in case tomorrow comes, which it has a habit of doing, we should not let care for the future take today away from us right now.

Stop over-thinking and worrying, start experiencing, NOW!

What are you waiting for? Something to happen? Like what? Someone else to do something that is important to them, not necessarily yourself? Nothing worthwhile will happen for you unless you make it happen. Live now, enjoy life, enjoy this moment, it's all that there is, **tomorrow is promised to no-one**.

As an example, some years ago my wife and I were looking forward to retirement after two busy lives of hard work and achievement. We planned to do this and do that, go here and go there, generally to relax and enjoy the so-called "Golden Years" together. Our plans were made and an equally busy retirement together beckoned enticingly. However, just after her retirement my wife was diagnosed with cancer and died a year later. We had done none of the things we had planned to do. None of our planned activities came to pass. Nothing we could have done could have avoided it, and it demonstrates that we do not, and cannot, control our lives, we can only experience them and to attempt to do more than that will only lead to stress and anxiety. The message within this experience, I think, is to live today to the full, don't put things off until tomorrow, love today. The experience today is worth far more than the regret tomorrow.

We can only control the moment, this moment, and the rest is purely chance and out of our hands, although we try, vainly, to control it and from which springs much of our frustration and unhappiness. We can at best exercise only some small influence on our life. Tomorrow is promised to no-one, live it today.

When you started reading this book, this line was in the future. This line is now here! What have you learned since you started reading this book, how really engaged with it have you been? Engaging with it or just reading it, watching the pages drift by; is this how life is for you, observing life but not really engaging? All too often we put off doing today that which we believe can be done tomorrow and thereby avoid engaging with our own life. Do today that which can be done today, there will be plenty more to do and enjoy tomorrow.

Time is a critical element in any change or transformation process. Time is life - don't waste life – life itself is a terminal illness, we know from the day that we are born that we are definitely going to die, we just can't be sure when. We all tend to assume that our death will be much later, some time in the future, not now, not soon, but we can't be sure.

Which line are you on in your page of life? Time to pay attention and to start living?

Some of the best examples of people who have taken this point seriously are those who have been diagnosed with a terminal illness of some kind. For them, there is now never going to be enough time and so they use what they have left to best effect, completing things, achieving things, packing more things into their life than they would ever have thought possible without that foreshortened deadline. Everyday, every hour, every minute is a blessing and something to be valued and made use of, enjoyed, celebrated even in the shadow of their own demise. They understand the finite nature of the time that we have to live on this earth and how glorious it can be if we take a positive attitude to it, they **focus** on what they can still do, not on what has already happened.

Of course, some may be reprieved from the early end and continue living on what, to them, is a new lease on life, but they almost always have been changed by the near miss experience and continue to extract the most they can from the time allowed with a clear focus on what is to be achieved. They noticeably live a fuller, happier life than those who have still not seen the importance of time. Why don't we copy them and enjoy life, every day, to the full.

Focus.

As we have discussed, dreaming will achieve nothing, we have to actually apply ourselves to this process if we are to escape from our prison. To escape we need to have a plan. When we have a plan we can focus on that plan to achieve our aim. See Chapter 4 for more detail and Appendix 1 for help with planning, there you will find a list of questions and suggestions that you will find useful in determining what it is that you want to change and what you want to achieve and by when. As part of that exercise we create a **timeline**.

Timeline.

It might be useful in terms of encouragement to do a quick timeline to show how clear our thinking is, or isn't, at this point, which will give us an idea of how useful the planning will be. To do this simple exercise only requires a piece of paper and a pen or pencil – it doesn't get much easier than that does it? With the paper in front of you placed lengthways, or "landscape" view, left to right, draw a line right across the page about half way down the page. Regard the left hand edge as the date you were born and the right hand edge as the day you will die. For the purpose of this exercise assume a life span of 90 years or whatever figure you feel comfortable with.

Put in dividing marks on the line across the page in equal portions of ten years and then another, bigger mark where you are at your current age on that line, so if you are 45 years old and you chose 90 as your lifespan your marker will be half way across the page. So now you have a line divided into nine sections of ten years each with a larger mark to indicate where you are in terms of life to date.

Below the line make a list of all the things that you want to see and do and achieve in your life, also possibly things that you want to change (locations, jobs etc), places you want to go to and so on. Number them and then on the drawn line across the page put a marker with the relevant number from the list that you have just made to indicate by when you wish to have achieved this objective. You will quickly see how much you need to do and in what order you want to do them if you are to achieve your goals. Interesting isn't it. More on this in Chapter 4 and App.1.

There is always a sense that we should be doing something else somewhere else, doing something NOW – this is just a distracting thought, an attempt by our mind to look at something more interesting, something shiny and glittery that easily pleases a superficial attention. What we are planning however is not superficial and we need to focus.

So, what else do we need to think about to escape our prison while we are creating the plan?

Put On Your Oxygen Mask.

Put on your oxygen mask. What? Where do I get an oxygen mask from and why would I need one? Well, let's think in terms of a figurative oxygen mask, not a real one. When flying with an airline there is always a safety briefing conducted by one of the cabin crew before take off. (notice how few people actually pay attention to it! Do you?). As part of that briefing they cover the eventuality of the passenger's oxygen masks dropping down from the overhead stowage in the event of an incident and they tell you what to do with them. Can you remember what they tell you to do?

The briefing tells you that you should not only put yours on immediately but that you should do so before attempting to help anyone else with theirs. Now, that is counter intuitive for many people, particularly for those travelling with children, because it sounds totally selfish, why would they say something like that?

The logic is perfect, in fact. In the event that the aircraft cabin should fill with smoke, for example, if you are trying to help children put theirs on first it may well be that you could yourself become overcome with the smoke before completing that task, you may then become unconscious, your children then without your help could suffer the same fate which could become terminal for you all. Even if you succeeded in helping the children first you could still suffer the same fate and then in the event of a successful conclusion to the flight the children would be alive but parentless.

Whereas, if you take the few seconds to put yours on first you have ensured that you are alert, alive and able to help others around you to the best of your ability. You are now part of the solution, not part of the problem.

20

Why do I draw this example? The reason is that in everyday life it remains as valid as it does on an airplane. We frequently get so involved with helping others in our life such as family, friends, colleagues, that we wear ourselves out, become tired, even ill, perhaps depressed or stressed and our level of support begins to diminish over time as we exhaust ourselves either mentally, emotionally or physically. Consequently, we then fail to perform at our best in our own world, either at work or within the family and as a resource for others to draw upon.

So what I mean by putting your own oxygen mask on first in everyday life is that we need to take care of ourselves first before giving time, effort and resource to others. This is NOT being selfish, it's just common sense. Take some time out every day for yourself, some me-time. It doesn't have to be a huge chunk of time, just some quiet moments when you can relax, do your own thing, not someone else's, free from interruption from anyone or anything, and yes, that does mean the 'phone/Twitter/Facebook et al as well. By being, and remaining, rested, calm, content and clear of mind you are in the best possible position to achieve your own aims and to provide the maximum sustained support to others.

We shall be returning to this theme in more detail in Chapter 5 entitled "New Life, The Journey". Sufficient to say for now that you need to take **responsibility** for your own welfare and well-being – and put it first, possibly for the first time in your life?

Responsibility.

I make no apology for returning to this theme because it is so central to all of our lives and yet many of us will have been running away from it seemingly forever and thereby limiting what we can possibly achieve, or trapping ourselves in a cycle of dependency on others.

To be clear, we are only responsible for our own life, not that of our partner, nor our parents or friends or colleagues although we may like to assume those responsibilities. I am solely responsible for myself and no none else (unless I choose to be for young children) and no one else is responsible for me no matter how much we may share our lives. And the same applies to you and to all of us. We may share our lives with others, we may consult with others, we may feel that we make joint decisions with them but we do not, we individually make up our own minds on every issue, every moment of every day and act accordingly.

It is true that very often our decision is to do nothing, to simply carry on as normal and we feel that we have thereby avoided responsibility for making a decision. But make no mistake, deciding to do nothing is itself a decision that we make. To avoid or not make a decision, as we believe, possibly because we feel that it is too difficult and we don't want to be responsible for any decision, is to actually make a decision not to decide, it's a conscious act to do nothing.

We cannot avoid it but we often either feel that we have either avoided responsibility or have shared it with others; we have not, we have just closed our mind to the act of deciding and attempted to share the blame, if any, for the outcome with others or with that mysterious other called "life".

"Life" is not a valid excuse for not being responsible for ones own life. There are no valid excuses. How often have you heard people say such things as "If only I had been born to rich parents my life would have been so different" or, "I can't help it, it's the way I was brought up", or "It's what everyone does isn't it?". These are all blatant attempts to avoid personal responsibility for our own lives, attempts that fool no-one except ourself. Again, how often do you hear people say things like "I don't mind" when asked even a simple question such as "Would you prefer tea or coffee" or "Shall we go for an Indian curry or a Chinese meal"? The phrase "I don't mind" translates as "I don't want to be responsible for my own wellbeing". This is a typical example of someone allowing life to happen to them rather than taking control and being responsible by which means a more pleasant outcome might arise.

This mental avoidance of responsibility is well demonstrated in the story of the man who everyday complains to his workmates about the contents of his sandwiches in his lunch box, always moaning about "oh no, not cheese again". One of his colleagues challenged him about this by asking why he didn't get his wife to make different sandwiches. What wife he replied, I'm single, I have to make them myself!

As previously stated, these type of excuses, such as blaming "life" are only valid whilst we are still young and are under the control of others. Once we reach the age of maturity – WE

HAVE A CHOICE! Do I stay here/keep doing this/follow the pack or do I take responsibility for my own actions and actually DO something to exercise control over my life. However, to make decisions, to take control almost inevitably means **change**, changing our ways, changing our location or friends or job – and don't we just hate change?

Change.

AAAARGH ! The "C" word. It's enough to frighten the horses. It is quite natural to want to live within our comfort zone where everything is familiar, routine, non-threatening, we know where we are at all times, we don't need to think about anything and we certainly don't have to make decisions and take responsibility for them. Let's just keep everything the same is the silent mantra that we live to.

Even when the familiar is not as comfortable as we would like we still hang on to it because at least it's familiar and therefore better than the unknown which might take its place if we make a change. We go to great lengths to maintain the status quo, fearing change, even compromising our own integrity to maintain it.

I recall intending to move house once and when the neighbours were told that we were moving one responded "oh, you won't like it there, it's very cold on that coast". Further conversation revealed that they had never been there but only that they had "heard" that it was cold. Translated into truth, what they were saying was "Please don't go, we don't know who will move into your house and we don't like/want change". They had attempted, probably quite unconsciously, to influence my life, quite naturally and understandably, to maintain the status quo of their own life, to avoid change. A small example but very typical of the way that most of us behave in order to avoid changes in our life.

Yet change is constant, change is inevitable, change is all around us and within us, in fact, change is the only constant in our life. We can't avoid it, resistance is useless and yet we fight it and try to resist it to the bitter end, and that produces tension, anxiety and stress which makes us ill, and that in itself produces an unlooked for change in our life which is worse than that which would have been made had we just gone along with it.

Change is only acceptable to us normally when it is imperceptible. Take a look in a mirror, you are very familiar with the face looking back at you but it is a very different face that looked back at you ten years ago. Change has gradually taken place day by day, but because you have seen it everyday, the change has been imperceptible, until you compare yourself with a photograph taken some years ago for example. Then, when faced with the stark contrast the change again becomes unacceptable and we bemoan the ageing process.

In preparation for our escape from the mental prison that we are in we need to overcome the fear of change, because it is going to happen anyway, and if we resist it we will necessarily waste time and energy worrying about it, often to the point of remaining inert in our comfort zone just to avoid it. However we do have **options** even within change. Confucius say – only the supremely wise and the ignorant do not alter. Which are you? Neither? Good, time to change!

Options.

Life appears to offer three basic options when we are unhappy. Option1 is to do nothing, just accept life as it comes, don't seek to influence it, satisfy our unhappiness through such things as comfort food, endless tv watching etc.. If we take this option we should not then complain about what life brings to us. We have done nothing to improve our lot, made no difficult decisions, rejected change as a matter of choice. Take what comes and don't bother everyone else with endlessly complaining about it.

Option 2 is to realise that we are not enjoying that which we have as a life and we consciously choose to move away from it in a positive manner, as a positive decision, a choice made, responsibility for change accepted. We may not know exactly what it is that we do want, but we do know for sure that we don't like what we have got and therefore any move in any direction away from our known dislike will bring positive change and the opportunity for improvement.

If you are standing at the North Pole and feeling very cold, walk in any direction you like, all directions go south towards the warmth from where you are standing. Change just one thing and further change must occur as the world orientates itself to your new reality, like a snowball rolling downhill gathering pace and size, becoming more meaningful day by day. Small change, or a succession of small changes are usually more acceptable to us than one big change. 100 is just lots of 1's, one hundred of them in fact, but they look very different.

Option 3 is the most positive and arguably the most difficult, but also ultimately the most rewarding. Often, Option 2 leads to Option 3 as a matter of discovery along the journey. Option 3 requires that instead of moving *away from* an undesired state that, instead, we move positively *towards* a desired state i.e. that we know what we want and move positively towards it. The only snag in this scenario is that it assumes that we know what we want from life in order to move towards it – and that's the tricky bit, knowing what we want.

Most of us for most of our life just go with the flow. Many of us end up doing at the end of our life pretty much what we were doing at the beginning of it, more or less, that is, nothing very much. Some of us, the lucky few, know from an early age what we want to be or achieve and go out and get it. They appear to others to be the exceptions rather than the rule. However there is no rule that says that we can't become the exception as well if we choose to be!

So, we have to discover what it is that we want and that can be quite difficult and often involves a few false starts. As the old Chinese proverb has it, be careful what you wish for lest your wish be granted. That is epitomised in the joke of the man who wished for a younger wife and the angels instantly granted his wish by making him immediately thirty years older, thus making his present wife instantly younger than him. Not quite what he had in mind presumably.

A second important lesson to be drawn from that is – be clear about what you want. Only when you are clear will you be able to achieve it. A well established saying is "If you don't know where you are going, how will you know when you have got there?"

Change: work with it, work towards it, welcome it, it is both necessary and refreshing – and inevitable anyway. Stop fighting it and thereby making yourself miserable. The alternative is to remain within your **self limiting beliefs** which define your comfort zone.

Self Limiting Beliefs.

No matter what circumstances we are born into, we reach the age of maturity with a collection of beliefs about ourselves which are basically founded upon the lessons learned from our parents, family, teachers and others around us as we grew up. Some of these beliefs are what we call limiting beliefs such as "I can't run fast", "I'm no good at maths", "I'm not attractive" and many are fallacious based as they are upon other people's opinions of us rather than our own experience. The problem can be that the opinions of others are so deeply ingrained within our thinking that we actually ignore our own real experience, experience which may well demonstrate clearly the mistaken nature of our belief.

When our personal experience does not fit our long held limiting beliefs we tend to dismiss it as a one-off, a fluke, pure luck or something similar. Not to do so would challenge our belief, a belief which is familiar to us and with which we are comfortable and to challenge it means that we have to make a change and take responsibility for the correctness of that change and, as we have seen, we don't like doing that. So we stay as we are, comfortably believing that we are shy or no good at maths or too fat or whatever.

Another way in which we gain mistaken impressions is through our own subjective experience rather than our real experience. For example, for many years I held a true belief that I was not good at the logical sciences, physics and chemistry but that I had a natural ability in human sciences such as Biology. Because of this, early in my adult life, I avoided job interviews which required more logical applications and only applied for those jobs that had a more subjective element to them.

It wasn't until I was in my thirties that my parents, during the course of a de-cluttering exercise, came across and gave to me all my old school reports. Imagine my surprise when, sometime later, out of curiosity I looked at them and discovered that throughout all of my secondary school years I had repeatedly and consistently scored high marks in Physics and Chemistry and quite low marks in Biology – the very reverse of that which I had held to be true for so many years. How to explain this?

When I thought it through I realised that the teachers of Physics and Chemistry had seemed to me to be rather intimidating, demanding teachers and that I hadn't enjoyed the lessons, whereas the Biology teacher had seemed to me to have been a warm and supportive person to me, probably because she recognised that I needed help and encouragement. Consequently I looked forward to and enjoyed the Biology lessons and carried forward into life with me the belief that I was quite special in this subject. A totally false belief, honestly held, but one which later limited my career choices at a critical time.

Perhaps the most damaging form of self limiting beliefs are those that I call the "musts", "should's" and "oughts" of life. The un-holy trinity of the English language, as I call them, are killers. When you hear yourself say one of those three words I suggest that you should do one of two things, or even both!

One, do just the opposite of the must, should or ought and two, ask yourself this simple question: Who said? Who said I must, should or ought to do that? Why "must" I, why "should" I, why "ought" I?

All too often the answer is that only "I" said that I must, should or ought, no one else. Self imposed pressure is the worst kind when using these words. Putting ourselves under pressure can be very productive and inspiring, it can make us achieve things that we never thought for a moment that we could achieve. It ensures high standards and performance and demonstrates desire and motivation, all of which are positive.

However, put a must, should or ought in front of the intention and it transforms it from a positive to a negative. No longer something we want to do but now something that we feel we must, should or ought to do, a complete turnaround. Example, I would really like to come for a run with you this evening but I ought to finish this job. Ought makes it a duty, not a like, makes it a task not a pleasure, makes it an imposition not a choice. I am giving up something I want to do for something that I feel I ought to do.

As a result of following the must, should or ought we may also now start building resentment against this imposed duty, this inconvenient task as it has become and if we are not careful, and we often aren't, we can project that resentment against the innocent recipient of our attention as though they had imposed this "ought" upon us. Sometimes they have of course, sometimes others do genuinely take us for granted and expect us to repeatedly put their interests before our own but it is OUR CHOICE that we do so, no one else's. They can only expect, only we can choose – our actions are our responsibility, not theirs.

All to often however there is no expectation from anyone else but ourself, we impose these duties all to easily upon ourselves for many reasons, including positive ones such as love and genuine care, but the end result is the same, stress, resentment and other negative attitudes which detract from our day to day enjoyment of life.

I remember a time in my own life when I learned this lesson of the musts, should's and oughts. After my father died my mother lived alone some little distance from my own home and as she was becoming aged and infirm I decided that it was my duty to care for her needs and so every Sunday morning I would drive over to see her, make sure that her house was OK and that any small things were taken care of.

This went on for some years until I noticed that I was driving there like a lunatic, in a bad mood and resenting the time that it was taking from my weekend when I had so much else I needed to get done in my own, now very busy, life. As a result my visits, I realised, had become visits from a *dutiful* son, not necessarily a *loving* son, there's a difference. As a consequence I was not enjoying the visits, actually resenting the time that they took, and I feel sure that my mother wasn't enjoying the time spent with this person, ostensibly her loving son, who was always in a rush and never in a good mood and who never had time to sit and talk with her. Overall the whole thing had deteriorated into a poor experience for us both. Why? How, when the intention was so good?

The reason why was that my life's circumstances had changed but I hadn't and I was trying to do something that was appropriate in the past but was no longer appropriate in the changed circumstances of a busier life. As a result the visits had changed from being a "like to do" to being a "ought to do", a duty, an ought, a must, a should and I resented feeling that I had to do it. Who said? Who said that I had to do it? Who said I ought to do it? Who said that I must do it? Who said that I should do it?

Me, that's who. Just me.

My mother had never said that she expected me to do it. The rest of the family had never said that I ought to do it. Only I had taken it upon myself to do it and then allowed it to descend into a must, should, or ought with the natural consequence that I built up resentment against this inconvenience and mentally blamed my mother for having to do it.

When I realised this (what an insight!) I changed my routine to fit my new circumstances and instead of the regular duty call I took to dropping in at odd times when convenient to myself on various days. As a result my attitude was better, my mother was able to enjoy the company of a son who had more time to talk to her each time and I was freed from the burden of expectation loaded onto my own shoulders by myself. I accepted that it was my choice to take this responsibility and therefore it couldn't be a burden, it just needed re-arranging to suit changed circumstances. How many such false "expectations" have you created for yourself or are carrying around as emotional baggage weighing you down and limiting your progress?

Girls in particular are outstanding at this trait, forever putting everyone else first, partners, parents, children, friends, pets, strangers; just anyone in their orbit is put ahead of their own interests thereby creating a an endless list of things that "should" be done before they can possibly take care of their own personal interests. Heroes all.

Finally, as I have mentioned before, we become trapped by fear, particularly fear of failure. What will people think if I don't succeed? People will laugh at me if I don't pass the exam. I'm not as good as my older sister, better not to compete because I will only fail. And so on and on go the negative thoughts, always negative, always restraining us, never letting us go. We learn to understand that we are not the best, or that it's not worth the effort because we are only going to fail anyway. Best to just muddle along, keep our head down, then we can't fail because we won't have attempted anything. What a way to live our lives but that is exactly what we do to ourselves.

My attitude is that not only might I fail but that <u>I intend to keep on failing until I succeed.</u> As the old saying has it, the man who never made a mistake, never made anything. Failure is not to be feared, we only learn from our failures and mistakes, we learn nothing from our successes believing they have occurred as a result of our natural talent and thereby take it for granted.

Some years ago I was addressing a meeting of business people in America who had never met me before and who were considering a joint venture together and, as recommended by their advisers, they were considering me for a senior consultancy role. They wanted to know who I was, what had I done, what experience I had such that I was to be the leader of this team. Well I gave them the usual boring presentation of my background which, while worthy, was hardly designed to set the world alight and then I got to the bit that I was nervous about.

Some years previously I had started a company which had only run for about three years and had then folded. In my own mind this had been a failure, I had failed. I did not consider that this was anything to boast about but in the interests of integrity I felt that I had to tell them the bad news as well as the good news.

Imagine my surprise when upon hearing this, the meeting came to life. Now I really had their attention – but, interestingly, not in a negative way! They were really interested about my failure and wanted to know more, and that's when I learned the lesson not to be afraid of failure. This group were not interested in my successes, they took those for granted. I would not have been there in the first place, they reasoned, if I couldn't demonstrate significant success.

They wanted to know what I had learned from my failure. The fact that at some point I had failed told them that I had got real, worthwhile experience behind me, I had "been there" just as they had. My mistake told them that I knew what it was like to really run a business, to lay awake at night worrying about the team etc. They knew, more importantly, that after a failure I had picked myself up, started again and gone on to more success, I had the spirit to succeed, that's why I would make a suitable partner.

They valued my failure and discounted my successes because they understood the key message – we only learn from our failures. Our failures are just part of our journey, not the whole journey, just learning points along the way when we pause and reflect before moving on once again but now more knowledgeable, more experienced, more mature. Feel the fear and do it anyway is a current phrase that fits the bill.

"I can't make decisions" is a commonly heard lament. Nonsense, anyone can make decisions and do make them all the time. We say that we can't make them because we are afraid that we might get it wrong and be judged by others thereby, again, becoming "other" not "self" referent and thereby a prisoner of other's expectations.

I subscribe to the view that there are no good or bad decisions, only consequences. Most decisions that we face could just as well be made by the toss of a coin, either way it landed it wouldn't make a great deal of difference which choice we made. Some decisions are more important and have greater consequences but there are very few decisions that are either life-critical or irreversible.

As a young manager I faced this problem myself, I wanted to get things right, to be well thought of, a safe pair of hands (other peoples opinions again) and to gain promotion. Unfortunately my reluctance to make decisions, my need to analyse everything before doing anything made me look slow and instead of receiving the looked for praise I began attracting criticism until one day my boss took me to one side and taught me the lesson.

The lesson was that getting things absolutely right wasn't necessarily the key criteria, making timely decisions was the key criteria. I questioned this by saying, yes, but what happens if, in my rush to make a timely decision I make the wrong decision, and he said, "Well, if you make the wrong decision you will quickly see that and that will show you what the right one is and, if you are making decisions quickly enough, you can change it before any harm is done". The contrary was that if I took a long time to make decisions and still got them wrong then it would take me an equally long time put it right, by which time it might be too late to avoid unwelcome consequences.

Very few decisions are irreversible, very few are life threatening and in that case there is very little to fear in making them. People say that when faced with some decisions there are no good options, that all options are unacceptable. OK, in which case we still have choice. In that case take the least worst option. It is what it is, deal with it. Feel the fear and do it anyway, the expectation of getting things right all the time is unreal, we need to **manage our expectations** in order to face the world free from the stress induced by fear.

Expectation Management.

It is all too easy to set ourselves up for a fall and thereby damage our own self esteem. We try to achieve everything right now, this minute, this hour, this day and then experience disappointment when it doesn't quite work out like that. Disappointment can easily lead to disillusion and we give up before we have even started leading to more disappointment and another blow to our self esteem.

An alternative to that is that we may be faced with a big task and are put off by the sheer scale of it and are so intimidated that we don't know how or where to start, and so we don't. Same result.

Expectation management is all about being realistic, not being carried away by our emotions and thereby losing our judgement. Emotions tend to swamp our logical side and so if we are excited at starting a project or are fearful of our abilities to complete it, those emotions will cloud our judgement unless we exercise some self control and keep things in perspective.

When considering a major task I like to keep in mind the question "How do you eat an elephant?". Answer "One spoonful at a time". What seems an impossible task when viewed in its entirety is really nothing more than a long succession of small tasks, or changes. It is the perfect reminder that nothing is too much for us, we just have to break big tasks down into small tasks and even smaller tasks where necessary, it is the very essence of good planning. The longest journey is just a succession of small steps, each step being entirely manageable even if the overall journey appears daunting.

I am often struck by how even small tasks take more time than allowed because I have consistently underestimated them. Always in a hurry, I forget that before I can do part "A" of my intended task I may have to prepare it or do something to it that requires me to do something else first and so frustration arises. Good expectation management would mean that I would have thought it through before charging in.

To avoid frustration, anger, low self esteem, we need to think things through calmly, plan thoroughly and execute the plan such that we meet our pre-planned expectations and feel good about another completed project.

Control.

It is natural to seek to control our life, indeed, many of us seek to control not only our own lives but the lives of others (this is not the place to deal with that particular problem). When we seek control we are really trying to minimise the effect of the surprises that life can bring to us, maintaining our comfort zone just the way we like it. Consequently when life brings us a surprise we feel out of control and immediately seek to restore the "normal" state.

We also spend a lot of time worrying and "what-iff"ing about things that may never happen, anticipating trouble, creating plan B (and plans C – Z), creating mind-pictures of what people will say or do in a hundred different fancied scenarios which never come to pass, all to maintain the illusion of control. In truth we can control very little of our life, there are too many factors working on us every moment of every day to control anything other than our own actions, which are often in response to new surprises whose appearance in our lives we couldn't control.

If the Meteorological Office using some of the most powerful computers in the world cannot forecast tomorrow's weather with absolute certainty what chance do we, as individuals, have of forecasting our own life tomorrow. How do we predict the traffic delay on the way to work that makes us late for an important meeting or that the boss is off sick when you need a critical decision from him; can you control those? It's back to unrealistic expectations which lead to negative emotional conditions.

Seek to control only that which you can control, deal with the rest. We cannot control everything, some would say that we only have control over our own actions, everything else is random. When we try to control or change that which we do not have control over then we again move into stress, be realistic. You may be aware of the best known three lines from "the Serenity Prayer" attributed to Reinhold Neibuhr 1892 1971:

"God grant me the serenity to accept the things that I cannot change; the courage to change the things that I can; and the wisdom to know the difference".

Finally, when we look at changing and becoming who we really wish to be, don't be afraid of the opinions of others, it's your life, no one else's. Leave your old self behind without a thought, as this little story illustrates.

A Monk and his disciple were travelling on their journey when they came to a ford across a muddy stream beside which stood a beautiful young lady dressed in satin slippers and beautiful silk gown, unable to cross lest she get her lovely clothes soiled by the mud. Seeing this the Monk approached the young lady and, lifting her into his arms, carried her across the stream and set her down on dry land on the other side. Later that evening at supper the disciple questioned his master thus, "Master, why, when our holy order does not allow us to commune with women, did you pick that lady up and carry her across the stream?". The Monk replied "I left her back there on the bank of the stream, why are you still carrying her?".

I close this section with another "prayer" which may provide some perspective on that which we have been saying so far and provide insight for the rest of this journey. It's called the Gestalt prayer as it takes it's theme from the school of Gestalt Therapy, which among other useful themes, encourages us to see things not as isolated events or issues but within an overall perspective, the whole Gestalt – our Life.

Gestalt Prayer.

I am I and you are you.

You do your thing and I do mine.

I wasn't put on this Earth to meet your expectations and

You weren't put on this Earth to meet mine.

If we should meet and get along, that's great,

And if not, it can't be helped.

Enjoy your life.

Chapter 3 – Rebuilding self.

If we are to leave so many outdated and now unwanted habits and behaviours behind, what are we to put in its place? We must set about rebuilding for the new you, and the new you requires equally new and different understandings and so let us look at some perspective, some context for what we are doing, let us explore the whole Gestalt.

A Neutral Universe.

I have commented along the way that the universe is neutral, that it doesn't care if we live or die, whether we are rich or poor and that we are therefore free to be who and what we wish to be. I can understand that some people, who may feel that they have had a poor deal in life so far, may take issue with that point of view. Not to accept that point of view, however, condemns us to believe that all of life is pre-ordained, that we are helpless victims of fate, doomed to live out this existence as it is dished out to us, unable to alter or improve our situation.

That would be to believe that Option 1, i.e to sit still and do nothing, simply to accept one's fate, in the Options section of the previous chapter, was the only option open to us, and yet even I was able to envisage, and set out, at least two other options, so one has to question the validity of not believing in the neutrality of the Universe. If life is not pre-ordained then we must take into account the element of human free-will, the ability to change our life and influence our destiny.

I like the explanation of this quandary which was related as being the difference between free will and Karma, or fate, as being like a game of cards. The hand of cards that we are dealt (when we are born into this world) is fate, we can't do anything about that. However, the way that we play those cards is free will and our relative skill in playing them can influence the outcome of the game (life), win or lose.

I am who I am and who I am is a function of my past, my upbringing, my social conditioning, my parental genes and many other factors, none of which I can change. But regardless of all of those factors which are outside of my control I can still grow and develop, modify who I am and my experience of the world around me, no matter what happens to me or how old I am. It is never too late to learn, I can change my future – how exciting is that?

I choose to ignore the saying that you can't teach old dogs new tricks. I believe that you can, as I prove every day of my life, and that the dog in the saying just chooses not to learn them and settles instead for the comfortable existence and the guaranteed meals without further effort. Lucky (lazy) dog!

And so, I am who I am by choice. I choose to be active or lazy, I choose to make the effort or to laze, I choose to learn and grow or to settle for who I am right now. Many of us blame our background for where we are today quoting early poverty or poor education as the reason why we are not more influential or richer or happier. And of course, where we are today is used as a perfect excuse for why we cannot ever be different – it is pre-ordained. Rubbish. Try Options 2 and 3 and see how very far you get and how much life can change. It is just convenient to blame the world for our own shortcomings, our own laziness, our own unwillingness to accept the challenge of change. There are many examples of "famous" people who have overcome very humble or modest backgrounds to succeed to great wealth and fame despite their background, that could also be your story.

I have met many people who were moving to another part of the country or even a new country to escape the perceived unfairness of their present situation. Phrases such as "I am not appreciated here" or "People don't like my sort here, I'm too clever/talented for their liking and I am being kept down", I'm moving to where I shall be valued more" are typical of the reasons given. Oh dear.

I am reminded of the book title "Wherever you go, there you are" (Wherever you go, there you are, Jon Kabatt-Zinn, Hyperion, New York, 1994) which, as a phrase perfectly states the problem. If I were to move tomorrow to Canada, Australia, Japan or anywhere else in the world, I would have to take myself with me, and with me goes who I am, my personality, my attitudes, my responses to life and the world around me and guess what happens next? Wherever I am, I am me, I am just the same as I was in UK and people will still react to me in pretty much the same way, and soon I will be moving on again and blaming where I have been for not understanding me – again. The world isn't going to change to suit me, I must change to suit the world or deal with the world more adequately to suit the way that it is. And only I can change me. It's time to accept and grow.

Positive Mental Attitude.

When thinking of what lies ahead in our journey of transformation it is well to remember the invaluable saying, attributed to Henry Ford, founder of the Ford Motor Company; "Whether you think you can or you think you can't, you're probably right". What he was meaning was that our mental attitude, note, our mental attitude not our mental capability, dictates whether we achieve things or not. Any situation, approached with a positive mental attitude, will be more rewarding, whether successful or not, than if it had been approached with a negative mental attitude and will have a higher probability of success.

"Positive Mental Attitude" has become something of a rather trite phrase, often used but rarely thought through or used in practise deliberately. Positive Mental Attitude has nothing to do with being either overly pessimistic or overly optimistic but rather of being a realist. Given that the Universe is neutral, if we approach a task positively we will, at the very least, take some pleasure from the very act of fulfilling the task (it not being a must, should, or ought) and our attitude will enable us to also take pleasure from expecting a positive outcome and, in the event of failure, to not beating ourselves up as a result. A win, win, win situation.

If on the other hand we take a negative mental attitude we will not enjoy the task, have pessimistic expectations and be unfulfilled at the end. Why bother? We have a choice in which attitude to adopt. We all probably know someone who is never happy unless they are moaning about something. Would you prefer to spend time with that person or with someone who more usually looks on the bright side and is happy to be alive. Which are you? As the old joke has it, if you don't know someone like that, it's probably you!

Another example would be to ask, is your glass half empty or half full? How do you view the world? Whether it is half full or half empty the amount remains the same, it's just your perception that sees it differently. How much more positive and affirming to see it as half full and give thanks for that than to see it as

half empty and complain about it. It is what it is, accept it grace-
fully and deal with it for what it is, nothing more.

Self Esteem.

A lot of our attitude towards life, as previously described, is a
direct result of our beginnings in life and our upbringing or mental conditioning. Had it been done more formally and with intent
we would be describing it as brain washing! Back to self limiting
beliefs. One quite amusing example of this which I used endlessly with patients in getting them to work through a difficult situation was in dealing with a question in which the answer given
was "I don't know the answer", to which I invariably asked the
next question, "If you did know the answer, what would it be?"
and then listened as the blocked or repressed answer came
tumbling out. We know so much more than we give ourselves
credit for, so much talent and ability locked up and unused inside
ourselves because we don't believe that we know, or can do, or
are not worthy enough to answer, even to ourselves.

This of course touches upon our own self esteem or self worth,
more phrases which through overuse have become almost
meaningless in conversational terms but which sit at the very
heart of our ability to effect the transformation that we seek. Self
esteem is an expression of how we see ourselves, which is why
the power of positive mental attitude is so relevant to all that we
do. If I see myself in a negative way I am less likely to believe
that I can do something than if I see myself in a more positive
way and I am therefore less likely to attempt anything, to keep
my abilities repressed in case "I make a fool of myself" by not
succeeding or by getting the wrong answer.

Positive mental attitude translates into confidence; do I feel confident in doing something based upon my beliefs about my capability to do so. Am I likely to make a good try at something or
simply hold back for fear of failure or embarrassment at not doing a good job? Am I likely to interview for a job for which I have
no previous experience but feel that I would like to do, relying on
confidence in my own ability to learn, adapt and grow into it or
do I not do that and stay in the warmth of my comfort zone which
make no demands upon me?

The opposite to self limiting beliefs are self-helping beliefs, the
beliefs that say "I can" and "I will". They break down barriers and

remove obstacles to growth and success. I often hear people say things like "I'm too old to do that now" or "I would do that like a shot if I were a bit younger". Let me ask you a question. If you didn't actually know how old you are, how old would you feel? Very few people feel older than they actually are, most of us feel younger but behave according to what we "know" (our real physical age to be) and not to how we feel and thereby limit our actions and choice of options for the life ahead.

This is most clearly seen in the context of health care. Doctors and therapist see quite a lot of cases where the issue is purely psycho-somatic, that is, purely in the mind of the patient. There is nothing physically wrong with the person except that they believe that there is, and so the belief becomes reality. This is the opposite of the placebo effect whereby Doctor's will prescribe a harmless, inert, pill for some condition to fulfil a patients demand that he "do something" only to see that the patient's belief in the placebo "cures" the complaint.

I had a very switched-on physiotherapist local to my psychotherapy practise who would, on a reasonably regular basis, have cause to refer one of her patients to me as, although the patient exhibited physical signs of an ailment, there was nothing actually physically wrong with them. Usually, after one or two sessions of psychotherapy, not physiotherapy, the patients shift in perception about their world was enough for them to shed the relevant stress load or anxiety which was causing the muscle tension leading to their physical condition.

We make judgements based upon what we think we "know" and in accordance with the value that we give to that knowledge. By not knowing we remove barriers, if I don't "know" that I can't do something then I will give it a go if I assign to it a high enough value to make the effort worthwhile. If I "know" that I can't do something I am unlikely to attempt it and to give myself an excuse I will assign that task a low value in order that I don't beat myself up about not doing it. "I could have been a brain surgeon, I just couldn't be bothered". Blow into your own sails, no-one else will.

Reassigning Values.

Life has no meaning other than that which we assign to it. On the face of it, an outrageous statement and one that is difficult to explain without getting into the whole God thing, which I don't propose to do here, although I will return to this theme and deal with that issue later. Let me give an example.

Let us, for the purpose of this example, assume that you know two people. The one on your left you know as an occasional acquaintance that you meet in the village pub once a week amongst a group of friends. You don't know them well, you are amused by their sense of humour but don't agree with many of their views. They are not very important in your life.

The other person, the one on your right, you know very well, have known them most of your adult life, they are a senior figure in your field of interest and have been a mentor figure to you for many years, helping you, and you respect them enormously.

Now assume that both of them learn of something that you have done and both respond by saying the identical words in identical tones and inflexions, "you are a fool because of what you have done". Think of the effect those words would have on you as spoken from each person.

The first person, because they are only a casual acquaintance and because you can easily disagree with their views as you have before many times, I suggest would only be a source of minor irritation, you wouldn't really care too deeply what they thought although perhaps annoyed that they should express it openly.

The second person, about whose views you care deeply, would, I suggest, wound you deeply with their comment, you would be horrified to think that they thought that of you.

Why the difference? The difference is in the values that you have assigned to the two people. The first person, whom you did not hold in high regard or importance, you, for example, quite unconsciously gave them a value of say, five out of a hundred. The second person who you held in high regard and value you assigned a value of ninety out of a hundred.

Consequently when they made a wounding comment they were able to hurt in you direct equivalence to the value that YOU had given THEM. In themselves their opinions have no value or difference except in that which YOU ASSIGN TO THEM, and you assigned different values. The first person can't really hurt you because you have not given them the value/strength to hurt you. The second person can hurt you very deeply indeed but only because you have given them the ability to do so in the value that you have assigned to them.

The same could be said, of course, in reverse. Their praise would have an effect, again in direct proportion to the value that you have placed on their opinions; the first person's praise might please you but wouldn't be taken seriously, the praise of the second person would fill you with pleasure and possibly pride at the thought that that was what they thought of you. Assigned values!

We do this all the time in all aspects of our life, sometimes we call it prioritising as we opt for which tasks to complete and which not to. Getting to work on time might be given a higher priority than reading the morning paper before we leave for work for example. The point being that just as we have assigned a value to someone or something, so we can re-assign a value up or down to suit new circumstances.

We need to revisit the values that we have assigned to all the important things in our life, relationships, priorities, objectives, if we are to make progress in transforming our lives in order to become more comfortable with ourselves in the way that we are living our lives going forward. Some values/priorities will remain exactly as they are, others will be reassigned higher or lower values dependent upon the view that we take of what we are trying to achieve. Some relationships will have to take a back seat perhaps as we begin to put our own needs first, or at least to emphasise them more. Others will take a higher priority as we choose to develop them to help us with our plans.

Remember, it's our life, and only we can change it positively. Our life is no-one else's and theirs isn't ours. We are not responsible for anyone else's adult life although we may choose to help where we can and if reprioritising people leads to them criticising us then we must accept that as a consequence, not blame. Bear in mind that when we make ourselves constantly available to others, doing everything for them we are not just pleasing our own ego by feeling useful we are, at the same time, denying them the opportunity for their own self expression, growth and development. Selfish? Just back off a bit and see how people do cope without you (your interference?) and you, and they, will be surprised at their abilities and how much time you free up for your own activities.

If you find that difficult, think of it this way. I often ask people's opinion on issues that I really don't need anyone's opinion on. The people I ask are pleased to give their opinion because they wish to help and feel good about being asked to do so, in this context I have given them an opportunity to feel good about themselves. Still feel selfish? My younger brother when at a loose end would sometimes come round and help me tidy my garage without my having to ask him. Excellent you may say, except that I didn't really want the garage tidied and would often return things to where they were later, but I had allowed my brother to feel useful and a good Samaritan. Don't stifle people, let them do their own thing without your control, theirs is their life, let them live it and grow within it.

I will return to planning in much more detail in the next chapter but for now it is important to understand that without a plan nothing will be achieved, it will all remain a dream, a wish, an "if-only". The big difference between a dream and a plan is a timescale. A dream has no time by which it needs to be achieved, it will therefore probably forever remain just a dream, no more. A plan on the other hand has a timescale built into it by which the objective will be achieved. Without the timing element, it's just a dream.

Perspective.

Falling back again onto folk sayings I recall the one that says that "You can't see the wood for the trees" meaning that we are so bogged down in the detail of the situation that we lose sight of the overall objective, that which we are trying to achieve. Often this is very true of our lives. We become so preoccupied with the day to day stuff that we lose sight of the fact that we are supposed to be living this life, not just enduring it. While keeping our jobs and paying the bills is important we also need to find time to smell the flowers and pat the dog, to see the bigger picture and enjoy our life, the one that we are working to support.

It is very common for people in careers to get sucked into working extremely long hours on a regular basis, never take holidays and generally become a workaholic and overlook the fact that their children are growing up without them, their partner is about to divorce them and all the fancy job titles, expensive cars and money in the bank won't change or replace that.

Only by re-assigning values will they correct the imbalance in their life and begin to enjoy it. Slavery was abolished a long time ago, why volunteer for it? Get a life, get some balance, step back a pace and see what's happening, wake up and smell the coffee, get real, whatever. I like the image of the fly landing on the television screen. What do you think it sees from that prime seat of the house with its many faceted eyes? The best view of the picture? Nope? Its way too close to see anything other than a blur; if it flew back and landed on your head it would have a better view, just until you swatted it that is. Step back from the day to day stuff, get some perspective.

In therapy, when patients came on a regular basis they would almost always choose to sit in the same place in the room every time although there was a wide choice of seating. As a deliberate policy, after the first two or three sessions, I would ask them to change places to sit in another seat. This gave rise to uncomfortable feelings in many patients, they felt that they were being pushed out of their comfort zone and being unsettled. I did this for a purpose, they were being made to see things, quite literally, from a different place or position, gain a different viewpoint, being jolted out of the familiar, to gain a different perspective. It was highly effective.

Perspective, or context (the whole Gestalt), is vital if we are to both enjoy our life and progress with our natural growth and development and not lose ourselves in the petty detail and the mundane of life.

We often feel that we have to be perfect, to do things perfectly, to look perfect and behave perfectly, be the perfect partner and so on. That way lays madness! I have never in my life, not once, ever met a perfect person (present company excepted of course). We are born imperfect (except in the eyes of our parents, who should seriously reconsider their values and standards), remain imperfect and die in the same state. Why strain for that which is not attainable? Just another imposed belief from our past tutors. A saner way would be to give everything our best shot, do the best we can such that we have nothing to apologise for or feel guilty about, but perfect? I don't think so.

Have you heard about the 80/20 rule? This states that we usually get things about eighty percent right at the first attempt and then spend eighty percent of our time trying to get the other twenty percent right.

If we look at the statement, that we get most things eighty percent right at the first attempt, we can see immediately the futility of straining to get the last twenty percent right and thereby using up a disproportionate amount of our time for diminishing returns. Sound familiar? I am not suggesting that near enough is good enough in all circumstances (you might argue with your brain surgeon who propounded such a view) but that we should think through more carefully how we use our time and whether we could be using it more usefully to achieve other objectives that might have greater value to us. The message is I think, don't beat yourself up trying to be perfect, just do your best and live with the outcome, after all, there is nothing else that you can do once you have done your best, anything else is just stress, self induced stress and we definitely do not need that.

Which brings us neatly on to habits. Much of our behaviour, and the thinking that creates our behaviour, is purely habitual, routine, almost unconscious in its nature, endlessly repeating old patterns that have worn a groove in our mind until our reactions are no more than knee jerk reactions to circumstance, requiring no conscious attention or thought. That is dangerous, especially so if we are to change our way of life or make changes in our search for personal growth and development. The older we become the more set in our ways we become, we have learned what we like and believe that we know what we believe so it is likely that our responses to any given circumstance are largely ritualised, almost devoid of any conscious consideration or thought of any kind. This then is the norm against which we must fight if we are to change and continue to grow and move on with our life.

Any norm however can be modified by the conditional phrase (one of my favourites) "at the moment". This phrase makes everything temporary, not fixed, and allows for change to be considered and to take place. Nothing is permanent, this is this for now - but it might or could be something else later.

An example might be that, following a slight illness recently, I changed from cow's milk to Soya milk as a matter of necessity. Having used cow's milk all my relatively long life this was something of a jolt and a hiccough in my established routine. The slight illness passed but I have never returned to using cow's milk, now preferring the taste of the Soya alternative.

Cow's was the norm, then, it isn't now. Soya milk is the norm "at the moment", ask me again next week, who knows, I might prefer goats milk? I use this to illustrate that no matter how old the habit of thought or usage there is no reason why it cannot be reconsidered and changed to fit new circumstances and for the change to be enjoyable. It is the same with all of our habits, we just need to be aware of them and the way in which they may be limiting us as we morph into the person that we can be.

So, we have now considered some of the ways in which our present thought processes and resultant behaviours may inhibit our development. Being aware of them we need to continually ask ourselves the question "Why?" or "Why not?" whenever we find ourselves thinking negatively about change and keep drilling down with the same questions until we reach rock bottom and we are satisfied that we can go no further when the decision as to whether or not to change is clear.

However, before we set off on our exciting journey we must be clear about what it is that we doing and where we intend to finish up, after all, if you don't know where you are going, how will you know when you have got there? We need a plan.

Chapter 4 - Planning for The Journey.

To those of you who are not reading this book as a continuum but merely dipping in and out, this section can be left until another time when you have more direct need of it as it deals with the process of planning the journey of change, rather than the journey itself which continues in the next chapter.

This chapter is not intended to provide a complete framework for personal change, there is a whole industry devoted to that and such guidance can be easily sourced, rather this is intended merely to raise your awareness and deepen your insight into what is required of you for effective change and you may then choose to begin to do-it-yourself or contact a professional coach dependent upon your own personal level of commitment and need.

DISCLAIMER. Planning is a common theme in many activities, sports, business and life itself. As such there are many common processes, techniques and methodologies in use around the world, none of them are of my origin. I have merely selected a small number of common techniques that the reader will find both useful and easy to follow. I make no claim as to authenticity or origin and all credit is given to any original author. Each one as described may be found easily on the web in the public domain and additional material can supplement these basic explanations. Now, on with the planning part of the journey to be free and to be ourselves as we wish to be.

There are some very simple and straightforward things that we can all do to prepare a plan to achieve any goal, whether it be a short term minor objective or a long term career or lifestyle change and I will explain these and also provide some simple forms in Appendix 1 to use as worksheets or simply to help you clarify your thoughts.

To escape the prison of our minds we need to have a clear understanding of what we need to do, where we intend to go in life, what obstacles are likely to be in our path and how we intend to overcome them and to have a desired outcome clearly in our mind.

It is a very unusual person, for example, who simply jumps into their car and drives aimlessly about without any idea of where they are going or why. We normally have a good idea of where we are going, how to get there and what we are going to do when we get there. It is the same with life. Left unplanned it is a haphazard journey that may well finish up in the wrong, or at least an undesired, place with nothing of any value at the end of it.

Many will be deterred at the thought of consciously planning anything in detail as they may infer that it might involve commitment, rigidity and relentless effort to the exclusion of all else. Not so. We know that, to misquote Robert Burns, the best laid plans of man often go astray.

Anyone involved with the armed services will know that the best battle plans often go in the bin following the first shot fired in battle, that it never goes according to plan! You can plan as much as you like, life will throw in many more unpredictable items than you can possibly foresee. A plan is just that, a plan, and plans need to be flexible to take into account new information as time goes along and amended accordingly. Any plan is only the plan "at the moment". It would be a huge mistake to stick rigidly to the original plan if it were found that the original circumstances on which the plan was founded had changed completely, it would require that the plan be amended.

So, a plan is not set in stone, rather it is written in pencil with a healthy supply of erasers to hand for amendment along the way. Any plan is better than no plan, no plan is just a dream. So, what do we need to know before we can start setting out our plan for the journey to the new me?

Firstly, what is it that we are trying to achieve, what do we want? We need to be specific in order to be sure that we achieve it. For example, if I said that my objective is to be rich, what does that mean? We need to define rich; does that mean ten million pounds or dollars, one hundred million, what does rich mean to me? And by when do I want to be rich? This year, ten years time, by the time the children leave school? When, specifically? April the 10th 2030 would be specific; "soon" would not be, for example.

Also, what is my motivation for this, why do I want this, what will it do for me, what will it look like or feel like, what will I be doing when I have achieved this, and where? And who with? The clearer the picture that we have in our mind the more likely it is that we will achieve our aims. Write down exactly, or as precisely as you can, what it is that you are searching for, trying to achieve or change – and why. Know yourself, understand your motivation, clarify it from being a vague wish to a clear intent.

When looking at plans we apply the **SMART** test to them to ensure that they are practicable, reasonable and achievable. **SMART** of course is an acronym and stands for **S**pecific, **M**easurable, **A**chievable, **R**ealistic, **T**ime-bound.

Specific means that we have refined our thinking to ensure that all the vague woolliness has been eradicated and we are left with a very specific goal e.g. I want to have one million pounds in the bank in five years from this date. That is specific. Now we need to apply the rest of the **SMART** test to it.

It is Measurable because we have a specific amount required by a specific date not some indefinable measure such as "rich" or "soon".

Dependent upon our circumstances it may well fail the Achievable measurement, for example, if we are only on a small salary with no expectations of advancement or inheritance.

It would also fail the Realistic measurement and so at this point we would go back to the beginning and reframe the objective more realistically or conjure up some money making scheme to meet the objective.

Being realistic, let's amend the amount to ten thousand pounds in the bank in five years from this date. That still passes the Specific and Measurable test and now we can look at the Achievable test again. Ten thousand in five years means we need to save two thousand pounds a year. Hmm. Let us assume that that is just about achievable, now we need to look at the Realistic test.

Is it realistic to believe that we will actually make those savings? If we can make these savings without too much effort then we can pass straight to the Time test but, If we can only just about do so, it means that we may be compromising other things that we like to do, or not be leaving ourselves any margin for error and again, we might like to re-examine the amount to be saved and start again. Let us assume that we choose to continue.

The time test is simply one of checking that we have very specific timings in our plan, particularly for completion. We might choose to insert other timings, for example, ensuring that at the end of the first year we have two thousand in the bank and four thousand at the end of the second year, and so on. Remember, without a time commitment, a plan is just a dream.

What we have done so far is enough to get started with a reasonable plan in place that we have thought about, clarified, made specific and understandable with clear goals. Now we have to think about how we intend to achieve this plan.

Firstly we need to assess what our assets are, what do we have to help us in our escape from our present way of thinking and life and that will contribute towards achieving the escape plan? Well, the main asset – is yourself! You are all that you have or can depend upon for certain. As we have said before, the responsibility is yours, no one else's, no one will do it for you. However, we do have other resources and we need to consider what they are.

Other assets that might help us might include our family and friends, colleagues, contacts and, dependent upon what our objectives are, such intangibles as our ability to borrow money, borrow office space and suchlike. Should we be enlisting these peoples help, and in what way? How can they help us? What do we need them to do (perhaps just encourage us)? Who else do we know that could be of help? Do we need to acquire any new knowledge or skills before we can start?

Then we need to consider what might go wrong with our plan and consider what actions we can take to minimise the risk or to enhance the probability of it succeeding. Do I need to leave home? Do I need a better paying job? I set out a more comprehensive list of questions that should be considered in Appendix 1 under the title of The **GROW** Model. GROW, an acronym again for **G**oals, **R**eality, **O**ptions, **W**ay Forward.

Finally, on planning, do not be put off by the size of the task that you have planned. Remember, the question of how do you eat an elephant? The answer, one spoonful at a time. Break each task down into smaller tasks until they are manageable. And remember, the longest journey begins with the first step, so what is your first step going to be in the journey towards the new you? Is it a call to a friend, write a letter of introduction, making a list? What is it? More importantly, when are you going to take it?

These points and more are fleshed put in the Appendix and are merely summarised here. It may well be of course that you have your own way of organising these things, great, it doesn't matter how you do it as long as it works for you and that it is effective in taking you forward into your chosen future.

Chapter 5 - A New Life, The Journey

The journey to becoming the person that we want to be, and are capable of becoming, requires that we not only a have a clear idea of what we want and how we intend to get it, but that we have a clear and focused mind that is capable of supporting and maintaining the effort to do so. No problem, you may think, I'm up for it. Well, you may think so, and that may be part of the problem. What do you think, and whose thoughts are they that are going around in your mind, are you sure that they are yours? I can hear the reply now; of course they are mine, who else's thoughts would or could they be? Well, think of it this way. Is your mind the same as your brain? Your brain is that physical lump of flesh inside your skull, your mind is the sense of consciousness that arises from thoughts, where are your thoughts located?

Most of us have a sense that "we" are not our bodies, that somehow we exist within, but are separate from, our body, so that we have a brain which produces the sense of consciousness, our mind, and the third party which some deem to be a soul, or our infinite "self", which is the part of us that senses the world around us, directs the mind to perform it's various activities and experiences our life, Descartes "ghost in the machine".

Mind Control.

Returning to the original question, whose thoughts are these, we can now see that the mind, when not controlled by the self towards some specific objective, is, in it's under-utilised boredom, quite capable of generating a stream of thought composed of random images which may well catch the attention of our consciousness and distract it away from other more specific tasks set by the self. If we are to focus, therefore, we, ourselves, need to control the mind in order to ensure that we get done what needs to get done and not be distracted into daydreaming, for example, which is really just us paying attention to passing random thoughts; or worrying, which is just circular thinking around an interesting, but not relevant at the moment, point of interest. I shall return to the concept of mindfulness later in the chapter.

I would suggest that our mind might be regarded in the same way as alcohol. Alcohol is OK as long as you control it, but if you allow it to control you then you have got a problem. It's the same with our mind. If we control it's activities we get a lot done, if, however, we allow it to control us with it's random activities, we get very little done. This is often referred to as being able to concentrate, to focus or not.

Unfortunately, we are only taught to use our minds, not to control them and consequently we spend our lives responding to the random thoughts of the most bored but powerful computer in the universe, our own mind. Under-utilised with productive work it spends it's time distracting us with streams of thoughts, images, challenges, distractions and general nonsense which we, unfortunately, in our ignorance, take as commands, instructions or orders to actually DO something about this stream-of- consciousness rubbish. As a result we finish up distracted, anxious and unhappy.

This anxiety or unhappiness, if left uncontrolled and able to fester, often leads to depressive moods, inactivity, loss of motivation and general wasting of our life as we watch it drift by, seemingly our of control – it is of course ACTUALLY out of control unless we make the effort to take command. Expressed simply, our mind is our biggest problem – who's in charge in there?

By focusing, by concentrating we take command but, like any activity, if we are not used to it then it takes time and practise before we do so effectively. Just like taking up a sport, when we first go to practise our muscles ache, we are tempted to cut it short, it just seems so difficult; why am I putting myself through this are the sort of thoughts that are typical of the time. Later, when we have practised more and our muscles are more used to the new effort it becomes a pleasure and we gain in confidence and ability, and so it is with controlling the mind. Again, I return to this theme later under the heading of mindfulness, for now, we need to understand the link between our thoughts, the emotional responses that they generate within us which lead to our reactions and responses to the world around us.

I Think, I Feel, I Act - the Link.

Escaping the prison of our mind so that we can truly be ourselves relies upon our understanding of just what it is doing to us unless we prevent it doing so by taking control ourselves. When our mind generates a thought and we pay attention to that thought, the mind also prepares the body to act upon that thought. For example, if it generates a thought that frightens us it will flood our body with adrenaline so that, if necessary, we can run away from danger or fight the danger, often referred to as the fight or flight response.

This was really useful when we were primitive beings as there was a lot of that sort of stuff happening to us and a fight or flight for survival was a daily reality. In the modern world however we are less threatened by external events and the greatest threats to our wellbeing come from within, from our own mind. We still frighten ourselves on a regular, daily basis with thoughts of job loss, mortgage arrears, child wellness and so on. The mind/body relationship doesn't differentiate between these present day issues and the old threat of a wild animal eating us alive, we still get flooded with fight or flight adrenaline-style boosters.

That would be OK except for the fact that we no longer burn those chemicals off in running, as in running away, or fighting the aggressor. We sit still. We just sit still or at most pace around the room worrying, hardly the same as fleeing for your life. So now we have a mind that has worried us, a body that is full of chemical induced energy that has nowhere to go and we find ourself, as a result, in quite a state of anxiety.

The energy has to go somewhere and so we burn it off in two ways. Firstly in generating heat such that we literally sweat or experience hot flushes, perhaps even trembling of the limbs in nervous anxiety. Secondly, and just as importantly, we burn it off through worrying, becoming anxious, stressed, uptight and possibly very aggressive in our behaviour. One only has to think of road rage to see this exemplified. Drivers, frustrated by the traffic making them late for an "important" meeting, become emotionally overheated through their brains telling them that they are late, become aggressive towards the next innocent car that "gets in my way" and explode with rage; dangerous driving is the result, death possibly the final outcome.

There is a direct link between what we think and how we feel about that thought and, as a result, what we do about it, how we behave in other words. Our behaviour is driven directly by our thoughts about any given situation. However, as a result, if we change the way that we think about any given situation we will change the way that we feel about it and our consequent behaviour will change to directly reflect those feelings. If we think angry thoughts we will feel angry and we may behave aggressively; if we think calm thoughts we will remain placid and we will behave in a more measured manner.

The key, therefore, is to assume control of our thoughts and thereby control our emotions which will enable us to behave in a manner which is appropriate to any given situation. A self evident truth? Not really. Normally we are not aware of our initial thoughts, usually we first become aware of our emotions first and then the thoughts that follow that awareness, and those thoughts will now be thoughts that are supportive of, and reinforcing towards, the emotional state that we have created. In this case we are being led by our emotions and behaving accordingly with the logical process following on behind, but subject now to the aroused emotional state. Never try talking logically to someone who is really angry, they can't hear you, their emotions are in control not their mind. They will only respond to logic once the source of their anger is removed and the emotions subside.

Cognitive Behavioural Therapy (CBT) teaches us the ability to break the link between thought, emotion and response to help us respond more appropriately to the world and thereby receive more beneficial responses from it. After all, the world is like a mirror, it simply reflects back to us what it sees of us.

If we are always unhappy or angry the world will seem like an unhappy and angry place to us, if we are more of a smiley, happy person the world will respond more positively to us, and so we can change our world by changing our own behaviour towards it, to change the world we must first change ourselves. It was Mahatma Ghandi who said "Be the change that you wish to see in the world."

CBT is a simple structure (Example exercise at Appendix 2) that asks us to examine our thoughts about any given subject, to note the emotions that that thought gives rise to and then also to note the response that this arouses in us. It then asks us to consider an alternative, more positive, explanation for the original thought and compare the new emotions that arise from that new explanation and see the difference in the response we make. This allows us, through conscious practise, to establish a more positive way of thinking, to form a new habitual way of thinking that will help us to become more positive about ourselves and the world around us.

Once we do so the world will respond to us in kind, becoming a more positive and welcoming place in our own perception of it. What is there not to like about that? Try the work sheet on anything that is bothering you about your life and see the difference for yourself. CBT is not the universal panacea for all of our troubles but it is a useful tool to be able to use to free us from negative emotions or when we become stuck on an issue that troubles us.

This is a great step forward in improving both our thinking and attitude towards life and in increasing our chances of successfully implementing our plan for change in our life. We have spoken of having a positive mental attitude and the above process provides one way in which we can achieve this and, as a by product, improve our mental health and strength

Psychosomatic Wellness.

We often hear people talking about others who are not well and describing them as having "nothing wrong with them, it's all in their mind" or "he's a hypochondriac, he only thinks he's ill". Well, while it may not be true in every case there is a lot of truth in the sentiment and we describe this type of ailment as being a psychosomatic illness, that is, it's all in the mind and as a result of our believing something we become physically ill in some way to meet the belief. If I think that I am ill then I will become ill to meet the requirement.

Another common form of this is when we become over-stressed, perhaps at work or within relationships. As a result of this sustained stress we begin to experience physical symptoms such as skin rashes, loss of appetite, in extreme cases we may begin to lose our hair or become temporarily impotent. There is nothing actually wrong with us physically but our stress, a condition of the mind, begins to affect the physical body. Remove the stress and the physical symptoms disappear. The generation of physical symptoms is simply our unconscious mind's way of telling us, bringing to our conscious attention, that we are becoming unwell and need to do something about it before it gets any worse.

We see this most clearly when we go on holiday because we then relax having quite literally (hopefully) left our problems behind us. We enjoy ourselves and our mind becomes focused on where we are and what's happening right now instead of the past. As a result of relaxing we notice that our appetite and libido increases, our frown disappears and all is well with the world again.

What we don't hear so much about is such psychosomatic wellness as that, the opposite side of the same coin of psychosomatic illness. In the same way that we can think ourselves into illness so we can think ourselves into wellness, and this comes back to having a positive mental attitude about life, our cup is half full not half empty, and we can use CBT to help us with that if it doesn't come naturally to us.

Adopting a positive attitude makes us more upbeat about ourselves and our world, makes us more attractive to be around for others and generally enhances our overall wellbeing. Remember Henry Ford's saying, "Whether you think you can or think you can't, you are probably right".

If you think/believe you can't do something your state of mind will prepare you to fail, after all, that's what you expect and the odds are that as a result, you will fail, just what you expected, no surprises there, you knew that all along. If, on the other hand, you adopt a positive attitude, while it is no guarantor of success, it will enhance your experience, increase your chance of success and in the event of failure will help you to move on, try again or generally to just get over it as you will already be focusing positively on the next step. We have looked at positive mental attitude and CBT as a tool to use in promoting more positive outlooks but they alone will not sustain us in our journey to the new reality that we are seeking. For that, we need all the help that we can get along the way.

Tools.

Have you ever stood in a Supermarket unable to find one thing that you really need, going round and around the aisles, double checking where you have already looked, finally in desperation asking an assistant where it might be, only to have them obligingly, with a smile, point out that there it is, right in front of you? I know that experience only too well.

Well, in life we tend to be the same about ourselves. All too often we talk ourselves down and feel that we simply don't have what other people have to enable us to get to where we feel we would like to be. Discouraged we don't try, but more often than not we do have that "something" within us, we just don't know where to look and we have had no-one to ask where it might be or point it out to us.

Successful people use everything that is available to them to help them achieve their aims. These aren't necessarily big things or esoteric skills or great knowledge, often they are ordinary everyday things that are available to us all, it's just that we either don't see them or we don't believe that they are relevant either to ourselves or to our aims and ambitions. We believe that the difference between ourself and others is some form of gift that they have, an unnatural talent or unfair advantage; it isn't, it is usually a number of small things, almost insignificant in themselves, but which when added together make a big difference, often greater than the sum of their parts.

A good example of this is in motor-racing where teams spend hundreds of millions of pounds and dollars striving to gain an advantage over their competitors on the track. They endlessly improve the aerodynamics, the engine performance, the driver's technique and finish up with individual end results that improve the overall performance of the car by hundredths or even only thousandths of a second a lap. But when they add up all the tiny individual differences each redesign makes the overall change is sufficient to give them a winning advantage. No one killer change, just lots of small changes or adjustments – and that's what we are talking about when we talk about improving our own lives, lots of small changes or adjustments that will lead to us feeling and performing better than we do at the moment. As with the previous example of the elephant, so every journey is made up of thousands of small steps. The entire journey may appear daunting at the outset but each small step that make up the journey is, in itself, entirely manageable.

In many cases these small changes are known to us but, to-date, we have chosen not to implement them. Hopefully, with new awareness and motivation these will now become more relevant. Because they are known to us I will not be labouring any particular point, merely bringing them back to awareness, no more, whether they are acted upon is of course a personal choice.

Diet. Let's begin with an obvious one, diet. Yes, sorry, but it has to be faced. Our diet affects the way that we feel, for example it can mean that we can feel full of energy to get things done or bloated and sluggish and not wanting to do anything. I am not an advocate of diets, any of them, they are all so close to the trees that they fail to see the wood, as previously discussed.

There is no magic answer, the only sensible approach is that the less that goes in over and above that which we need, the less there is to burn off as energy or to put on as excess weight. Of that which we ingest we can choose to be healthy or choose to pork-out on cakes and biscuits, it's our choice, no one else's. So, you know what is healthy, you know how that compares with what you are eating so, what are you going to do about it? It's a matter of self respect isn't it? What we look like on the outside is a reflection of what we put in on the inside. The change will be different for everyone but the need is the same. You know what you have to do, the only question is when are you going to choose to do it?

Exercise. An even worse subject than diet to face up to, normally, but there are some things that we can do which are more acceptable to us than others.

Personally, it wouldn't cross my mind to go jogging, for example, I just don't like the look of intensity and unhappiness on the face of the average jogger to want to do that. Have you ever seen a jogger smiling? I haven't. Hot, sweaty, painful; not a good look. Team sports are not everyone's cup of tea either and many sports are very competitive which doesn't suit everyone, or they take up too much time and so the temptation is not to bother.

How about walking though? We all do it, it's quite natural, doesn't impose unnatural strain on us, we can fit it into a busy day, just walk around the office block at lunch time. Do similar things several times a day and breathing will improve which has the by product of improving our complexion through more effective uptake of oxygen.

Another is Tai Chi, a graceful, peaceful, low key exercise suitable for all ages and can be done in the privacy of the home or in a social group. Improves balance and co-ordination. Yoga is yet another with similar attributes. There are many others and any such low key exercise has the effect of taking us out of ourself and thereby induces peacefulness and relaxation.

So much for the body, what about the mind? If we regard our brain as a muscle then you will easily understand the concept of over tiring it, like any other muscle it needs to rest, switch off, wind down, relax, cruise for a while.

Meditation. It is not necessary to don saffron robes, shave ones head and go sit on a mountain top in order to meditate. A quiet moment in a comfortable chair, some time set aside in a quiet room without television, radio and other electronic gizmos bleeping and bonging in the background, perhaps some peaceful music to induce a light trance or daydream, give the cat some lap-time, relax in a bath while thinking of nothing; all these induce a sense of peace and calm and break off from the intensity of the day in order to re-charge the battery. It needn't take long, even five minutes will help, more is better.

Many of us will want to take it further and sit in a room with just a candle burning, or to chant or whatever it takes to gain some stillness in the mind. We talked earlier about controlling the mind and meditation can teach us one technique for doing just that.

There seem to be two schools of thought with regard to meditation; one talks of emptying the mind of all thought (which I personally find incredibly difficult) and resting in the void of nothingness. Perhaps that's for the more advanced practitioners. The other talks of not emptying the mind but of merely observing the thought stream, not acting upon those thoughts, merely observing them as though they don't belong to us, looking at them as though they were just so many TV channels and we are channel hopping, detached from them.

This I find much easier and when in everyday life I find my mind wandering I can remind myself of this and switch back to the channel I want to watch which is the one about what it is that I want to be doing. Practise makes perfect and so day dreaming can become practise for controlling the mind, how good is that? And it's free! I will return to this subject later.

Breathing. Breathing? Don't we do that naturally? Well, yes we do breathe naturally, but not necessarily effectively. We don't use it to help us, we just do it without thought (which is a good job because I can be forgetful these days). As one technique within my psychotherapy practise I would, from time to time, use hypnosis for patients. Part of the process of inducing hypnosis is to draw the patient's attention to their breathing in order to move their mental focus from the outside world to their inner world. As soon as I mentioned breathing their mind would noticeably, immediately take "control" of their breathing as though it hadn't been going on all day quite naturally without any help, and the breathing becomes more measured.

When we are uptight, stressed or anxious our breathing becomes very shallow, when relaxed it becomes quite deep, watch any sleeper breathing deeply or any person when they release tension as they let their breath out as though it has been an effort to keep it in, which it has of course. If we learn to breathe appropriately, i.e. become conscious of it, we can constructively use it to help us. Taking deep breathes when we are anxious will relax us, help us to think clearly and keep our attention outwards not inwards on our fears and thoughts.

Mindfulness. This is very much coming to the fore, almost a social fad or fashionable thing to be doing but nonetheless it has genuine benefits, although, as with so many other things it is not, by itself, the answer to the problems of the universe.

Mindfulness is the practise of focusing on the moment, this moment, and thereby isolating the mind from all the everyday cares and the random stream of thoughts that assault us every moment of every day. It is a combination of focused attention, meditation and appreciation for the whole experience of living based upon experiencing this moment, right now, whatever I am doing.

An example would be that frequently when we eat food, we do so whilst also doing something else such as watching television, talking or reading a book, listening to music. This means that we are not fully "present" in the moment, enjoying the food. We are multi-tasking, sharing our attention between several things, focused on none of them, merely going through the motions without fully appreciating any particular aspect of any activity.

To eat mindfully would require us to be doing nothing else but simply paying attention to our food, not just paying attention to the act of eating but focusing on every detail of it such as the way the food not only tastes but the way that it feels in our mouth and looks on the plate, to enjoy the feeling of chewing and swallowing, taking as much as we can from each experience and aspect of the act of eating. This is perhaps most easily seen when a knowledgeable person tries a newly opened bottle of wine. Before even tasting the wine they will hold the glass up to the light to examine colour of the wine; they will swirl it around the glass to see how it clings to the glass; they will sniff it to extract as much information about it through the nose as is possible and then finally they will taste it. In tasting it they will then circulate the wine around the whole mouth to touch all taste receptors to get a complete picture of it before then pouring it fully into the glass. Thier whole attention has truly been given to the single act of tasting the wine, that is mindful attention to the experience.

That is just an example but we can see that this is just what we don't do most of the time, always hurrying, always multi tasking, rarely fully appreciating any experience. Compare that with the occasional experience that we do fully experience because it stops us in our tracks and demands our attention, a beautiful sunset, a rainbow, a river flowing and so on. It is no accident that such experiences are natural ones for they are outside of our own puny, human capabilities and therefore matters of wonder and in that they provide us with some context for our own life and how we fit into this world.

The Natural World. We have spoken about peacefulness and the need for resting the mind but we also need to consider resting that which some refer to as the soul, our deepest inner self where we find meaning and relevance.

We can be happy, relaxed and seemingly content but somehow, there is often an inner craving that says, yes, this is OK but I need something more, something deeper, my soul is hungry for connection and satisfaction.

Mankind is extremely creative and produces beauty in many forms such as art, music, sculpture, buildings and many other forms which we experience around us. Whatever we do however is limited in some way, very beautiful perhaps but not entirely satisfying, not something we can personally relate to on a deeper level.To do that we need to have contact with the natural world, to be at one with nature if only for a short time.

Sitting on the shore listening to the waves, walking a hillside and feeling the warm breeze, these are the things that touch us deeply, that make the connection with the universe of which we are such a tiny part, that make us complete, and we need to find time for these moments.

Some will happen quite spontaneously like seeing a rainbow, others we need to take time out for and go and find them for ourselves. The more we do that the more we feel content and complete, happy on a very deep level because we understand that we belong to, and are a part of, something quite marvellous. Make sure that there are enough moments of wonder in life, we need as many as we can get, and share them with others, they will also need them as well. I saw a message recently that said "Happiness is contagious; go out and contaminate as many as you can". Excellent advice.

Chapter 6 - Self Management.

Before an important event it is customary for athletes to receive a last minute "pep-talk", a boost to the confidence, a hardening of resolve and such like. I have no idea if they work or not but I thought that it might be useful to throw in a few thoughts before we turn our attention to the journey of change, discovery, growth and development that we are intending to begin.

Understanding Self.

A well known management saying is that before we can understand others we must first understand ourself; before we can manage others we must learn to manage ourself and before we can develop others we must first develop ourself. A rather long winded way of saying "Put your own oxygen mask on first" but no less valuable for that.

We need to be aware of ourselves at all times, not in a shy, introverted way or the brash, over-confident manner of youth, but in a measured, evaluative manner, asking ourselves questions in checking our reasons for behaving and reacting to the world in the way that we do. In that way we will truly begin to understand ourself which in turn will help us manage and develop ourselves in a more positive and meaningful manner.

For example, we often point the finger of blame at others, often literally by pointing the hand, but more often verbally or mentally. Try this little exercise. Point the finger of one hand out in front of you as though pointing at someone. Now, continuing to point, turn your hand over so that you can see your other fingers. Which way are they pointing? Back at yourself!

For every finger of blame we can point at someone else we should always be aware of the three fingers pointing back at ourselves, indicating that we are also to blame for our misfortunes and that we are alone in being responsible for our own wellbeing and happiness, not others.That sums up the point that I am making. Before pointing the finger of blame make sure that you are yourself free from blame, guilt or association with what you are blaming someone else for. And even if someone else is to blame, what good does blaming do? Why not be positive and simply accept and move on, building your own world more positively.

If you are given to being judgemental of others firstly ensure that you are yourself perfect in all respects. We may not be guilty of that which we accuse others of but we will certainly be guilty of some other shortcoming which others would be quite in order to point out to us. People in glass houses shouldn't throw stones is a very apt saying. Blaming gets us nowhere, engaging a positive mindset on the other hand enables us to conserve energy, be productive and move on.

Blaming others is easy, doing something positive about it is much more difficult but it is the path of personal growth. Accept responsibility, be the first to act, acquire compassion for those less able or talented, act with integrity at all times, be the change in the world that you want to see.

Black or White Thinking.

Be aware of your own "black or white" thinking, that is, thinking in terms of absolutes; he's right, you're wrong, it's my way or the highway, it has to be done this way. Such thinking is very limiting in terms of learning and tends to give us a blinkered outlook and an attitude that can be off-putting to others, and we need other peoples help if we are to be successful in what we are doing.

This has nothing to do with focus and everything to do with attitude. No-one knows everything, although you will meet many who may think that they do. The world is not made of black and white elements, if it were then decision making would be easy because alternatives and priorities would be crystal clear.

The reason that life can appear difficult is because the way ahead is not clear, and it keeps changing and this makes life one mess of sludgy grey, not black and white. Being dogmatic about "the right way" or "the truth" simply exposes a lack of thought, awareness or understanding about the world around us and the way that it works which can lead to conflict rather than resolution, or sub-optimal outcomes as they are referred to these days. Look back at the section on CBT and practise seeing things from another point of view to gain a better understanding of almost anything.

To understand this point listen carefully to a Diplomat (NOT a politician) on the News when one appears and see how they express themselves. In their world, nothing, but nothing, is straightforward but everything is resolvable if only we can keep talking.

Diplomats are trained to accommodate all points of view without ever losing sight of their main objective. The skill is in leading all parties to believe that you have listened to them and that their interests are taken into account even if the chosen way forward is contrary to their advice. An object lesson in how to smooth over the spiky bits of life without getting hurt.

A good example of black or white thinking and relative truth is to imagine two people who have been to a football match, each a supporter of the opposing sides who played that match. Ask them about the match afterwards, this single event that they both witnessed in the same place at the same time together and you will get two widely different views, or "truths" about what took place in that event. One man's "skill" will be the other man's "luck" in their descriptions. How can that be? It may be because what they saw was biased or affected by what they believed to be the truth before they started, "my team is right and good, your team is wrong and bad". Absolute, black or white thinking leaves no ground for compromise, understanding or growth, it is a dead end.

Personally I "know" nothing. I do however "believe that I know" many things, but that is just a belief "at the moment", what you or others have to say on the matter may change my belief into a new truth or new belief. So, I have many beliefs or understandings but I know of no absolute truths, a truth is a black or white thing whereas a belief or an understanding recognises that it is capable of change and is not, therefore, absolute and finite. This leads to a much more constructive approach to life and conversations.

Scientists tell us that there are no absolute truths, only truths as we understand them "at the moment" in the light of current knowledge. Every day new research reveals new insight into existing truths which modifies them and new truths emerge to be taken forward until even more knowledge is discovered. Even the speed of light, long considered to be an absolute in itself, and certainly absolutely the fastest speed at which anything could travel, now appears to be uncertain.

While I have focused on black and white thinking there are many other ways in which we limit our potential by using poor thinking habits. For example, **negative filtering** - if we have a negative mind set we will inevitably see negativity everywhere which will limit our willingness to live our life fully. Simply flipping the logic coin will enable us to see the other side and think more positively and change our world for the better.

Over-generalisation or **catastrophising** matters will colour our view of the world. To move from "He doesn't like me" to "Everyone hates me" is but a small step of **emotional reasoning**, not logic. Quite frequently we come across a situation where someone has taken an innocent comment about a situation personally, assuming that we are in some way blaming them for a fault when we are merely complaining about the system, beware of **personalisation** in your life, don't assume that negativity is directed at you personally. **Mind reading** should be left to the entertainment industry with their stage acts and not brought into our everyday life. We do not know what anyone else is thinking, we cannot, but still we insist on believing that we can and acting accordingly, often against our own better interests. If in doubt, ask, do not assume that "I know what you are thinking". Of course there are the other two that we have dealt with in some detail, the **fallacy of fairness** and the **should, musts and oughts** of life. Banish them all from your thinking, they do not help and only breed negativity in your mind and your world.

As we have seen, we are often either oblivious to our own abilities or, if aware, we talk them down or limit them by our negative thinking habits. When we talk them down enough times we actually believe our own message and degrade our performance accordingly, even, as we have seen, refusing to attempt things because we "know" that we are no good at them and that is an absolute truth. Like the scientists, we need to question those apparent truths and find new ones, ones more representative of our actual qualities and abilities.

Rule of Three.

A little secret of life is the rule-of-three. The rule-of-three says that if we hear something three times, in the absence of anything to the contrary, we tend to believe it as the truth. This is the way that lies become truths and rumours become facts, particularly if the rumour or lie is repeated to you unwittingly by someone whom you trust. "I didn't believe it until Mary told me and if Mary says it's true then it must be true". Of course, now "knowing" it to be true the danger is that you repeat this new truth to a friend who now repeats the cycle, it now must be true because <u>you</u> told them it was.

This works just as effectively in our inner dialogue as it does in the everyday external world and so when we keep telling ourself that we can't do something it's not long before believe that we really can't because we no longer attempt it or, at best, attempt it expecting to fail, and we usually live up to our own negative expectations.

Of course, the opposite is equally true. If we hear repeated praise we believe the message – we are good at doing something. This is why repeating "positive affirmations" to ourselves help us achieve our goals

Stuck-ness.

Sometimes, when our internal chatter is all negative and the world seems to be against us, we just cannot see our way around a problem and our spirits drop and we come to a halt. At this point we need to have some reminders to tell us that this is not the end at all but just a pause in our progress.

When people go on diets and try to lose weight they often experience just such a pause in their progress after the initial excitement of losing a few pounds weight. I call it plateauing because progress hasn't finished, it's just levelled off for a time, and so it is with progress with all things. Typically weight watchers will lose a few pounds very quickly which is very encouraging, but after the first few easy pounds have gone the body seems to pause before continuing. It is this pause, when nothing seems to be working no matter how hard we diet, that puts people off and they think "Oh, what's the point" and give up. Had they persisted just a little longer the weight loss would have continued quite naturally as the body adjusted.

Stuck-ness, or plateauing, needs to be seen as being a time when we are simply gathering our resolve and strength for the next stage of our venture. Look at it positively with understanding (and CBT?) and it will be seen differently. Watch an athlete just before they explode into action, immediately before the record breaking takes place there is a pause, a gathering together of mental and physical resources, getting "in the zone", during which time nothing is happening, or so it appears to the watching world, but which is necessary if the best performance can begin. So it is with life. We are sent these problems to make us sit still and consider fully what we are doing, to review our performance and to steel us for the next event.

Remember at times like this we need to remember how our life can be compared to other natural systems such as the giant oak tree. We begin with the odds stacked against us, a small acorn must fight for space in the undergrowth. We must find the strength to dig in and put down strong roots, fight for the nutrients to sustain us and overcome a lot of competition for the air and light that will sustain us and to grow above all others, standing tall in the sunlight which is our reward for the sustained effort made over time. No quick fix will make it, no easy answer, just sustained effort slowly growing, pushing aside obstacles in our way, growing as we were meant to, growing towards the light of self knowledge, enlightenment and peace in our soul.

Just because we can't always see the way ahead, or the final destination that our efforts are taking us towards, it doesn't mean to say that it isn't there. When climbing mountains the summit is often not seen until the climber is almost there, being obscured along the way by lesser ridges and cliffs until, after a long sustained effort, the climber finally rounds a corner or crests a ridge and at last sees his destination and his heart is lifted by the sight; then, and only then can the climber truly understand what the effort was all for and how worthwhile it has been. Our life can be seen in just the same way.

Head vs Heart.

Inaction is a valid action, as in "don't just do something, stand there"! Decision making is something that many of us find difficult, even for everyday decisions there seems to be no clear and definite answer. Often we are torn between what we know we want to do and that which we feel we must, should or ought to do and we have dealt with that earlier. Another form of conflict is that between head and heart. This is a conflict between what we know logically in our head that we have to do and that small insistent voice from the heart, that *feeling* that, no matter what our logic is telling us, we want to do the opposite and we don't know why – but we do it anyway and it makes us happy to have done so.

We can refer to this voice from the heart, as opposed to the head, as instinct, intuition or just our inner, true person speaking to us. This inner voice is rarely logical, at least in the obvious sense, and seems to have no foundation in fact at all but we are rarely wrong when we listen to it. The problem is, we don't trust it because we don't know where it is coming from or what it is based upon and that gives rise to our inner conflict.

Having said that, (here comes controversy), females appear to be much more likely to listen to it and act upon it and learn to trust it than males are. We have heard the phrase "women's intuition" spoken, often unfortunately in a derogatory sense, as describing the ability to make leaps of logic such that we seem to arrive at the correct answer but cannot describe logically how we got there, we just "know in our heart" that it's right, and it usually is.

Learning to trust this inner voice, or knowledge, can be hard work if we are more inclined to be left brained (logical), than right brained (intuitive, sensing), indeed many of us never reach the point where we will listen and trust and we blank it out, others listen and act upon it quite naturally, trusting through experience that it is right. There are many occasions however when it only serves to confuse us as we fail to follow our instincts but also doubt our logic and so we remain in the middle, dithering.

There are many explanations for this inner voice. Sometimes it may be our unconscious mind picking up clues that, consciously, we haven't observed and putting two and two together in background and bringing that composite knowledge to our attention seemingly outside of logic. This is demonstrated most clearly when, after worrying about an issue for hours like a dog with a bone, we give up and do something else and the answer to the problem comes to us as a realisation out of thin air, usually when we are relaxing in the bath or just switched off mentally. That is an example of the brain continuing to compute in the background while we turn our attention elsewhere, the answer is entirely logical but we didn't witness the logical process by which we arrived at the answer and are amazed at how clever we are!

69

A more subjective school of thought suggests that we remember everything that has ever happened to us but we never bother to file the information in any sort of order, that our minds are like a huge junk room full of jumble and that sometimes, although our conscious mind cannot recall a relevant previous experience our unconscious mind can, it's been doing the filing all along but hasn't told us. Consequently, when we are faced with a decision, it is quite capable of nudging us in the ribs saying "This is the answer, listen, this is the answer" but it doesn't tell us what that answer is based upon so we don't trust it.

A third and deeper explanation is that of the "collective unconscious". Posited by Carl Gustav Jung and others, the suggestion is that not only do we know everything that has happened to ourselves we also know, or have access to the knowledge of, what has happened to all mankind through all time, the collective unconscious mind. It is suggested that we can tap into this knowledge and it surfaces as intuition. Who knows?

Sufficient to say that the inner voice of the heart can often conflict with the cold logical voice of the head and we need to recognise what is happening and choose which to listen to or we are doomed to remain in a dither. I quoted at the beginning of the book the piece of folk wisdom "Lose your mind and come to your senses", well, delete the word "senses" and replace it with the word "intuition" and it may have greater meaning to you. Ask yourself not what you *know* but rather what do you *feel* about a circumstance and the chances are that your unconscious mind will show you the answer, it will "feel" right. As engineering people will have it, if it looks right it probably is right, and there's no one more logical than an engineer

And so, having looked at a few issues that may hold us back, it's time to get on with our journey of growth and self development.

Remember, life itself is wonderful and all that we need to do to enjoy it to the full is to accept responsibility for our own life, to stop blaming others and stop assuming false responsibility for them and move along the road positively. We suffer when we don't accept responsibility and try to avoid the consequence of our own action. Acceptance of ourselves just as we are and acceptance of the world the way that it is is all we need to grow and develop.

Remember, it is what it is and I am who I am. Accept change as a natural part of life and just go for the ride free from attachments. Don't stand in your own light by creating futile resistance, instead, step out of your own shadow and become the person that you want to be.

If you could do just one thing to begin your journey today, right now, what would it be?

Do it!

Chapter 7 - Energy

Usage and Abusage.

We have spoken earlier about tapping into greater resources of knowledge than we were hitherto aware of, Jung's collective unconscious for example, and it is the same with energy.

When we think of energy we normally relate that thought to whether we feel tired or not, did we sleep well or not and are we motivated to get out there and get things done. We are aware that our energy levels vary dependent upon the time of day and whether we have eaten properly of not. Beyond that we really do not consider energy to be more than any another facet of our life which is either available in plentiful supply or not at any given moment in time.

Energy, however, is not as simple as our view of it and there is more to be made of that which we already have, and even more available that, as we are not aware of it, we do not use. It goes without saying that the more energy that we have, the more we can get done – if we choose to, and we now know all about choice and whose it is, don't we?

Assuming that we are determined on our path and wish to progress then the more energy that we put into our project the more successful we shall become and the sooner we will achieve our objectives. So how do we go about understanding what energy is available to us and how to use it most effectively?

Energy.

Most of us will understand the concept of energy management, the need to pace ourselves in order not to get over-tired or fade before the working day is done. Some of us are morning people, others come alive later in the day (night?), we are all different in the way that we use energy but how many of us are aware that there is a great deal more energy available to us than we accustomed to using?

The energy that we are normally aware of is the raw, physical energy that we continuously create. We have a natural store of energy within us which we expend upon our daily activities but which is continually renewed through our natural eating cycles. Our food is converted into energy and any surplus energy is stored as fat for later use – all to often however we never get to "later" and it remains stored as fat and we gradually become obese. This is not the time or place to wander off into the tangled thickets of dieting, weight loss etc. We all know what that is about; eat less or exercise more or gain weight, your choice, the rest is window dressing.

But that is just the raw energy that most of us are aware of. There is far more energy available to us however in more subtle forms which we can easily tap into in order to quite literally transform our lives, if we choose to. To tap into this energy we have to decide, to choose, to consciously explore these energies, to harness their powers for our own and the greater good. This might mean changing our ways, altering our lifestyle or even doing things differently, which is why many people do not even bother, being content to let things stay as they are, it being just too much effort to get more out of life and enjoy it more on a day to day basis. Now that truly is laziness and a waste of life itself.

This of course also impacts upon our positive mental attitudes, remember them?

We have already explored the concepts of positive mental attitudes and psychosomatic health which demonstrate the link between mental activity and physical well being. In very general terms there are three things that we can do with energy – conserve it, waste it or channel it.

Conserving Energy. In terms of conserving energy this can be either negative or positive. Laying on the couch in front of the television every night drinking beer and eating popcorn may be fun and may be construed as conserving energy but it isn't actually achieving very much except relaxation, which, while necessary in order to balance life up, needs something to balance against. In terms of moving forward in life it is, quite literally, a non-starter.

On a more positive note, conserving energy is the opposite of dissipating it and therefore to ensure that we are using it most effectively we need to be absolutely clear in our minds what it is we are trying to do and direct, or channel, it towards specific objectives.

If we try to do too much, if we have too many projects, if we take a scatter gun to approach to life our energy will be spread too thinly in any given direction and consequently will not be the most effective in the direction that we have chosen to go.

So, in terms of conserving energy we need to at least be clear in our minds what it is that we are trying to achieve and focus our efforts/energy on that particular direction.

We need to pace ourselves appropriately. Rome wasn't built in a day and our hopes and plans won't be achieved in a day either. We need to keep perspective on the reality of our workload at any given time and focus constantly on the main issues without being distracted by the many minor attractions that inevitably arise along the way.

Wasting Energy. Our natural energy constantly needs an outlet. This outlet, as described above can either be positive or negative and so, in the absence of choosing to create a positive outlet, the energy will itself seek the next best thing which may well not be in our best interests.

An example of this might be in an everyday occurrence such as our deferring doing a job until we have been asked or told several times to do it, at which point we become annoyed and the energy that could have been expended positively in doing the task is now misdirected and wasted through its emergence as irritation, or even anger, at being nagged to get it done. This anger is wholly negative and harms us physically by raising blood pressure, flooding our system with fight or flight chemicals and it harms us indirectly by showing others that we are not sufficiently responsible to achieve simple tasks without supervision, and so on and so on. Energy needs to flow, if blocked it will find an outlet not of our choosing and so the question arises of who are you choosing, or allowing, to direct your life; yourself by exercising positive choice, or others by avoidance of action?

That example reminds me of another old saying that is normally used in a sense of criticism, particularly applied to various workmen who have had to be recalled to put right faulty workmanship – why is there never time to do it properly but always time to come back and do it again?

To have to redo something is a waste of time and energy, to put it off is a waste of energy, time ticks away and energy is dissipated in a thousand little ways every day. The message is – focus, focus, focus. Do things that have to be done when they need to be done, and do them once only. The time and energy that this simple (?) practise frees up is enormous and feeds into our feel-good factor as we achieve more than we thought was ever possible in the time available. A rule followed by all carpenters is; measure twice, cut once. Don't waste energy by having to cut twice.

Channelling Energy. To use or channel energy effectively we need to be focussed on our desired outcomes and assiduous in our application of energy effectively. This in itself can be demanding and tiring to be so attentive to this one aspect of our life and so we need to consider what "tools" we have to help us in this important task.

Meditation.

Often misunderstood in the West, meditation is often seen as requiring endless hours of squatting in strange positions while staring at a lotus blossom or candle flame or some such off-putting nonsense. In truth, meditation is little more than focusing the mind on one thought, or lack of thought, in order to achieve a relaxed state whereby one can let go of the immediate day-to-day worries and gain some respite from the busy, everyday mind that we are all familiar with (yes, that one, the one that stops us going to sleep at night!).

Meditation requires no special bodily position or place to do it, no chanting of mystical mantras or any other difficult-to-believe-in practises. Meditation can also be seen simply as "zoning out" in modern speak, as in removing the attention from present circumstance onto something more conducive to our peace and tranquility of mind.

While this may offend the purists I believe that day-dreaming is one acceptable form of this where the mind is simply not where the body is, it's off on a pleasant walk through day dreams of it's own, relaxing without recognition of passing time – which is the big bugbear of our lives, always rushing to _be somewhere_ instead of relaxing to just _be_, always doing, never just being.

Meditation facilitates the change from doing to just being. We spend our days in a frenzy of activity, constantly rushing to meetings or meeting deadlines, following to-do lists with time limits on when and how we do it, ticking boxes of checklists off to follow and so on. Of course this does not end with the end of the working day.

We similarly fill our evenings with more checklists and to-do lists, housework, cooking, entertaining – in short, we are forever doing. No wonder then that when we finally get to bed our mind won't relax, let go and allow us to get off to sleep. It needs help to do that, and meditation can provide the help that it needs to allow us to rest, relax and unwind and, yes, to sleep properly.

Broadly speaking there are two approaches to meditation; the first is based upon the notion of emptying the mind of all thought and the second is based upon the notion of merely observing thought, the flow of consciousness, as it arises. The first may be too big a step for beginners while the Western mind may find the second more easily achievable with a little practise but it is very much a personal thing so do try both and make up your own mind as to which you prefer, there are no rules, it's up to you and your own preference.

Like any sport, exercise or routine, meditation needs a little practise before one becomes at ease and skilful with it so a little patience will go a long way and, by circular reasoning, meditation once adept, will help quiet the impatience of everyday life –that's what it's for!

So, what do we have to do to meditate? First of all decide upon a spot in which you will practise this gentle art. It does not need to be a mountain top overlooking snow covered hills or a lonely cave within which we can be cut of from the world entirely.

A quiet room, in the bath, inside your car parked in a quiet spot, sitting on a beach - anywhere that you can be quiet and not be disturbed by the influences of the everyday world is suitable for meditation. This means also that we need to ensure that we are free from that greatest of all modern problems, the beep, ping, ring and trill of communications devices such as mobile phones, tablets, vibrating wrist watches and so on and so on. Take them all off, turn them off or just put them somewhere where they cannot be heard, felt or experienced in any way. (That in itself is good medicine for the heart and mind in this manic world). Be assured that the world will continue without your expert guidance and input all on its own for at least half an hour until you are free to return and take the helm again.

Additionally, turn people around you off in just the same way. Ensure that the time taken for meditation is uninterrupted time so tell family or friends around you not to interrupt this time for any reason, even if the world is coming to an end in a favourite "soap" on television or the gas man wants to know where the meter is. Record the "soap" and let the gas man find it for himself, he's not helpless. If you seriously believe that your continuous presence is essential to the wellbeing of the planet or at least your family then you need a different sort of help, call the nearest Counsellor or Psychotherapist immediately.

So, we have a quiet spot and a freedom from interruption as preconditions for successful meditation. What else? Well, we need to find a comfortable manner of meditating. Be assured that there is absolutely no necessity for tie-ing yourself and your limbs in knots to achieve improbable sitting positions in order to achieve peaceful insight and calm. Leave The Lotus position to those who are more dedicated or practised and who can find further pleasure from it.

Whether you choose to sit in a chair or on the floor, buy a special meditation stool, lay on your bed or stand on your head is up to you. All that is required is that you are comfortable and safe and able to respond appropriately to any event outside your meditation place should it be necessary. Be comfortable, loosen clothing, do whatever you need to do to avoid distraction for the period of time that you choose to dedicate to this peaceful practise.

Whichever position you choose, don't be afraid to move about to remain comfortable, if you itch, scratch! Later, with more practise you will be able to control such things or at least ignore them but to begin with just relax and go with the flow and let it happen. If you don't attend to these small but irritating matters they will simply distract you from the task at hand.

Now we come to the choice of methods, whether to empty the mind or merely to observe the stream of consciousness as it parades in front of our mind.

To begin with either way may seem difficult and inevitably some frustration will arise but just keep on keeping on, practise really does make perfect. Let us take the first one first, emptying the mind.

Tuning Out. In our natural everyday state our mind provides us with a constant barrage of ideas, images, dreams, wishes, intents, memories, reminders, creations in a seemingly unending stream, the stream of consciousness. Unfortunately we tend to pay attention to this constant barrage of ideas as though the world would end if we didn't and we believe that each image or idea is ours and ours alone and that we must in some way act upon all of these impulses, hence our frantic lifestyles.

In truth, they are not ours, they do not require attention, they are not orders or commands and very little will happen if we selectively ignore them. Think of all these ideas etc as channels on a television and understand that we can channel-hop, ignoring the channels we don't like and only paying attention, or selecting, those that we do find interesting. Already you have made a start in tuning out from this mental "noise".That simple understanding itself will help you to reduce the noise and mental chatter that is a constant and no, it's not just you that experiences it, it's all of us. It's just that some of us become more practised than others in turning it down or turning it off.

In quieting the mind to silence, many people advocate focussing the mind on an object, say a crystal or a candle flame but any object will do, a pen for example or a cup, whatever is to hand. Based on the principle that the mind can only think of one thing at any one time we therefore choose to direct it at this object, or, as in the analogy above, select the appropriate television channel to watch.

By watching the object, or closing our eyes and imagining the object, we occupy the only available thinking space with it so that we cannot think of all these other things that the mind wants us to consider and so we become quieter and quieter, more calm and peaceful and so restful, allowing our mental batteries to re-charge.

Sounds easy doesn't it? There is just one snag. The mind does not like this singular focus and rebels by trying to distract us into considering all the other many more interesting and colourful ideas that it wants to present us with. This distraction, to begin with, is a constant and we have to struggle continually to bring our mind back to the object from where it has been distracted, and it will be distracted until we have sufficient practise to control it.

78

Eventually we reach the stage where the mind is still and then we can begin to tune in to more subtle awareness, the feel of the air, the sound of silence, how one hand is warmer than the other, how peaceful it all is.

Tuning In. The second method is to not attempt to empty the mind at all but to simply observe it going about its' business without becoming involved in the process, to be a watcher and not a participant, rather like watching a sports event on television, we can enjoy it without actually taking part. However, unlike watching the television which will excite us we simply observe our thoughts without allocating any importance to them, the outcome is not important and we have no interest in their content.

We are simply observing what is arising and watching it pass by, blending seamlessly into the next thought arising until that too fades and another appears in front of us and so on endlessly. We all too often accept our thoughts as commands or orders, important messages that must be acted upon right now when in fact they are simply adverts for what we could do if we so chose, but right now we choose not to and so they can safely be ignored.

Again, as with tuning-out, our minds do not like being ignored, they demand that we join them in their crazy, frenetic dance of ideas and images and so our mind will keep trying to distract us and get us involved in the whirl of changing scenes that it presents to us. The skill is, whenever we find that we have been distracted, and we will be until we get used to it, to bring our mind back to the original point of observance, a position of detachment and to keep doing that until the mind accepts that you do not wish to be distracted, that you are indeed a disinterested observer and nothing more.

Neither of these methods are easy to begin with, the ease with which you will be distracted may be disheartening but perseverance pays off and a little discipline in this respect will go a long way. There are no magical secrets to learn, no incantations to memorise (although chanting a mantra some say can help), simply sitting still and applying a little self discipline is all that it takes and the benefits in terms of peace of mind and tranquility of spirit can be enormously beneficial in all aspects of life.

Mindfulness.

Mindfulness is beginning to attract a lot of attention now in the West although, in truth, it is a concept that has been around, and practised, ever since mankind looked for peace and rest from the busy mind. Based upon similar principles to meditation it relies on the fact that one can only think of one thing at any one time and that by focussing upon one very specific aspect of life one can derive great benefit/enjoyment from it, more so than one would normally do whilst safely ignoring the frenetic world about us.

Mindfulness is all about living fully in the moment, about truly experiencing everything we do every moment of our life. As we have seen previously, if we spend this moment either regretting the past or fearing the future (which is what we are doing all too often in our mind) then all that we do is lose this moment, the one that we are actually living and can do something about – like enjoying it!

Mindfulness takes this several steps further however and creates a way of life which raises one's awareness of the real world that we inhabit and enables a greater enjoyment of every moment in life, adding value and intensity to all that we do.

An example of mindful living can be illustrated by the way that we eat our food. We eat food several times a day either at set meals or as snacks along the way during a busy day. However, whilst we enjoy our food we rarely focus upon it as a specific activity or even taste. All too often whilst eating we also talk to others, make phone calls, listen to conversation or the radio or television, read books or papers; many other activities often take place at the same time as we are eating and we therefore divide our attention between the various activities and, it is argued, not getting the most out of any of them because of our shared attention span.

We know that we are eating a tuna sandwich but do we really taste the tuna as a specific taste, separate from the taste of the bread or are we just aware in a dulled way that we are eating a tuna sandwich because that's what we ordered? There is a difference. A mindful eater would be focussing on each mouthful to the exclusion of all else, feeling the texture of the food in the mouth, sensing the temperature of the food, experiencing the taste of the various component parts and extracting as much sensory pleasure as possible from each mouthful, excluding any distractions such as music or conversation for example.

Compare that with your own everyday experience and you will see that most of us miss an awful lot, moment by moment as we rush through our days. This rushing, this multi-tasking, this rush, rush, rush, adds to our overall stress and anxiety and takes away a lot of the simple pleasures of everyday existence. Whilst trying to live a truly Mindful life is probably unrealistic for most of us, we can at least make an attempt to take from the principle some lessons that we can apply at times during our day, to genuinely slow down and smell the coffee – quite literally.

Alternative Sources of Energy.

We have looked briefly at what we routinely understand to be the main source of our energy and what we do with it. However, in addition to that which we create through the normal cycle of eating and living generally, we have far more energy available to us through other sources than we are normally aware of and I intend to touch upon one or two of those sources to reveal their application to our lives in order that you will find your own way to implement these, or similar, methodologies into your own way of life.

Many belief systems worldwide hold to the idea that all things in the universe are joined or connected in some way through a universal energy, an energy field that is all encompassing, benign, constant and is the very being of life. Western science is now beginning to add logical "meat to the bone" in finding such fields active within the human body. Given that this has been the basis of such practises as Acupuncture for thousands of years we might well say "about time too".

This energy is said to be within us all and can be channelled for healing purposes or released within ourselves to provide balance, stability and calm in our nervous/mental/emotional systems. Given the frenetic nature of life, at least here in the West, this would seem to be a positive contribution to our finding and using resources to accomplish our own aims in life; another small change that might add up to something greater than the part itself when used in combination with the other small changes that we have discussed so far in this book.

To attempt to summarise all the different variants of these beliefs or practises would take up more time than I have left on this planet (in this life at least), sufficient to say that I have used two of these "techniques" in my own life and practise with many patients and have seen demonstrable, positive changes in terms of health and happiness over many years and in many different circumstances. Let us take an overview of them merely to open the mind to possibilities either directly or through exploration of your own.

While our discussion to date has been about creating energy, these techniques are about releasing energy already within us that may be tied up in emotional or mental conflict and which is therefore not otherwise available to us. By releasing the negative aspects of the use we are freeing the energy up for more positive application in our everyday life and also hereby creating a healthier mental/emotional environment for up to live in.

Emotional Freedom Technique or EFT for short, one of several similar therapies or practises which make up the Meridian Energy Therapy family. It is loosely based upon the universal energy theory and forms the basis of acupuncture practise.

The theory suggests that the universal energy that connects everything is intended to flow into us, flow around us and then flow out of us in an uninterrupted stream back into the universe. Any interruption in this flow will lead to ill health of some kind, either mental, emotional or physical. However, interruptions can occur due to trauma, upset, stress and similar occurrences at which point we hold on to the energy to deal with the emotions arising from any such event, which in turn leads to a diminution in our overall health. Acupuncturists release this energy, or unblock it, thereby restoring health through the use of special needles inserted into the body at various points on the body.

EFT, instead of using needles which are invasive, uses a technique of tapping on the surface of the skin at similar points to create a similar effect, and very effective it is too. I have taught many people this technique thereby empowering them to take control of their own innate energy fields thereby creating wellbeing within themselves which is, of course, then conducive to further personal development.

There is a mass of information on this technique on the internet should you wish to pursue an interest in what is, after all, a purely benign and simple way of healing yourself from negativity and releasing that energy for more positive uses in your personal development.

Reiki. Again, based upon the belief in a universal energy, Reiki seeks to balance our personal energy field through the channelling of energy such that we are quite literally "well balanced" in terms of our own wellbeing and it can also be channelled for the purpose of healing others, a very worthwhile practise and one which brings many benefits both directly and indirectly to self and others.

The principal difference between these two practises, and there are many more, is that with EFT it is very easy to learn the basics oneself whereas with Reiki one needs to be instructed in this art form from the beginning. Reiki can also release/enable further energy within oneself through the generation of "spiritual" thinking and quite intense emotional releases, all of which are useful in redirecting energy in a more efficient and positive manner, thereby adding another small change to the greater sum.

These types of energy based practises provide many benefits all of which are beneficial if used properly and are another way in which you can explore your own potential, unblock old pathways and renew and invigorate your whole being. As indicated above, they can also feed into your overall belief system, religious or not, and enhance your daily experience of the world.

Chapter 8 - Inspiration for Life's Journey

Becoming All That We Can Be.

The journey of personal growth that we are now embarking upon will have a different direction and a different outcome for everyone, but it will also have one thing in common for everyone as well. That one common thing will be the conversion of personal knowledge into wisdom leading to personal growth.

We all know many things on many subjects but all too often this knowledge remains unused or poorly understood and, at best, undirected towards our greater interests and beliefs.

Knowledge only becomes wisdom when it is understood in the context of the wider world in which we live and is directed towards doing the highest possible good for the most possible people – service to the greater good, the wider universe, of which we are but a tiny part.

Selfish use of our knowledge, by which I mean use that is directed solely in our own personal interests, may help us in our day to day endeavours and careers but it doesn't necessarily help us to become a better person, a more rounded personality, a more useful member of our community, all of which are part of the journey that we are undertaking.

Carl Gustav Jung, one of the early, great original thinkers, along with Freud, of psychology said that our purpose in life is to become all that we can be and surely that is the purpose of our journey here isn't it? This is a theme that is reiterated in different ways in all the great religions of the world. What is meant by this?

In summary, the view is that in our early life we are quite naturally faced with dealing with the many challenges that life brings to us; those of growing up, making a career, starting and supporting a family, creating security within our life and protecting those for whom we choose to be responsible. That is easily recognisable as our everyday life and it occupies the first half of our life, dependent upon how one defines that.

However, having met those challenges with varying degrees of success, the view continues with the opinion that in the second half of our life we should lift our heads up from the daily grind and the pursuit of material wealth and goodies and begin to consider the bigger picture, the wider horizon of life, and reflect on how we can contribute, not just to our own material success but also to our emotional and intellectual growth, our contribution to the wider social group to which we belong, how to use our knowledge in a wise way to help others less fortunate, all of which adds to our own growth towards becoming a whole, well-balanced person, valued not just by self but by others.

This may be seen in giving service to others, in not being selfish with our material wealth, giving to charity, doing good work, contributing in many ways in the support of others around us, serving a higher purpose than the narrow selfish interests that we have served so far in life. It is in this that we begin to understand the wisdom in the saying that "It is better to give than to receive".

Strangely enough, this is a natural process and we see it in others and sense it in ourselves in many ways, unfortunately, not always in a positive way.

A good example of this is the so-called "mid-life crisis" which seems to afflict people in their forties or fifties. It is at this age that people begin to wonder about life and to question their own place in it and begin to sense a passing of time and the need to do things "before it's too late".

At this point people give up the jobs that they have worked so hard to get, kick over the traces generally and have extra-marital affairs or get divorced on a whim and generally behave in a quite uncharacteristic manner that is unsettling to all those around them, and, often leads to disastrous circumstances, all in the name of "starting afresh".

What such people fail to see is that it isn't necessary to start again, only to amend the direction in which they are travelling – that is the difference between knowledge and wisdom. In the first instance we use our knowledge, or lack of, to "start again", throwing away much of what we have in the process and in the second we use our wisdom to both grow through building upon that which we have already achieved and to develop ourselves through service to others, putting our own personal interests second in service to the greater good.

It is only natural at this point in our lives that we begin to seek meaning, purpose and connection with life, to see what we have already achieved as unsatisfactory or even meaningless because we are quite naturally turning our inner attention away from the material objectives of the first part of our life and quite unconsciously beginning to seek deeper meaning in the second part of our life, a different set of values and standards. Our values are changing in other words, it's just that we misunderstand this and feel that a whole new life is required to satisfy this feeling of being unsettled.

At this point we often describe ourselves as being disillusioned with life or needing a new challenge, being unfulfilled somehow, which of course we are as our inner needs morph into something more ethereal, more subjective and less easily measured on the scale of life's achievement.

But the use of the word "disillusioned" is a good one. Although we often use it in the negative sense as in meaning "dissatisfied" its' true meaning is more accurately reflective of what is actually happening to us.

To be disillusioned means to be freed from illusion, not to be dissatisfied as it is usually used. In this case, freed from the illusion of the value of material worth in the greater context of life itself. So we are freed from the illusion that, for example, money can buy happiness, that material wealth is everything. I have met many wealthy people who are just as unhappy as everyone else and their unhappiness remains with them until they discover a truer meaning to their life involving service to a greater good.

You will have noticed that I use a non-religious description, that of the greater good, rather than that of the greater God. If you wish to make them one and the same then that's OK, if you wish to avoid any hint of religion but recognise that there is a spiritual element to your make up then that's OK as well. If you recognise neither then you still have some pleasant surprises to come, and come they will. All we are interested in doing is finding our own truths.

It is the spiritual aspect of our being that takes us out of ourselves and enables us to gain a different perspective on the world, gain some context for our life, to see the bigger picture. When we are young, unless we come from a religious background, we tend to avoid thinking of the higher self, we are afraid of the whole "God thing", it's just too big for us to contemplate and really doesn't seem relevant to the modern way of life, there just isn't time for such introspection we tell ourselves. It is only in the second half of our life as we become more reflective about our own life that such considerations intrude, whether we wish them to or not.

Of course, as we grow older we become more aware of how much of our life we have already lived (wasted?) and how little, by comparison, we still have left to live. This tends to focus the mind tremendously and in doing so the bigger questions of life emerge, for example, when I die, what next? What has been the meaning of my life? What should I be doing for what remains of it? Should I be buying some "insurance" by starting to pray or go to church? How do I do that and will it work?

It doesn't matter if we don't have the answers (although some would claim otherwise) but we bother ourselves with the questions, and it is this bothering that leads to us focusing on our life and thereby precipitating, in many cases, the mid life crisis.

Why is a God or a Spiritual Being so necessary for us anyway, why are we even mentioning it here? Well, as the saying has it, if God didn't exist Man would have to invent him, and of course there are many who would say that that is exactly what has happened. It doesn't matter whether we have or we haven't, we still look to that Presence for salvation in hard times and inspiration in the best of times and quite involuntarily both pray to, and give thanks to such a presence in such exclamations as "God help me" and "Thank God for that" in moments of stress or relief. One very apt saying that arose from the slaughter of The Great War was that "there are no atheists in the trenches", meaning that under stress we instinctively seek help from a more powerful force than we have to hand.

Such thoughts of a greater power can be both inspirational and/or destructive dependent upon how we have acquired the underlaying beliefs. I have met many patients whose life and wellbeing has been crippled by the teachings of various established religions. The burden of guilt induced by the Churches, the resultant low self esteem and lack of self worth leads to stunted personal development and an inability to experience life to the full. Freeing people from such restrictive beliefs is to see individuals emerge from the shadows, standing tall at last, rather as one watches a flower bloom from a closed bud, blossoming in the sunlight, spreading itself to catch every possible ray of sunshine, *to become everything that it can be.*

On the other hand, a sense that there is something quite literally Divine about life can be positively inspirational and it is this sense of a greater presence, something higher to be aimed for, something to please (Note – to please (positive) not appease (negative) as in so many religious teachings) and be part of can inspire us to greater efforts and achievements, higher development and escape from the selfish self.

There is no art like a natural landscape, no music akin to birdsong on a quiet evening, no literature to match the words of love generated in the heart by nature itself, a oneness with something bigger than ourselves, a masterpiece created for our pleasure by an artist greater than any other artist past or present to remind us that love is a tremendous healer, binder and source of energy but above all - motivator.

We need this awareness to give us strength to complete our journey. An awareness of the bigger picture, a sense of perspective about what life is truly all about and how we need to transcend our own selfish needs if we are to truly become all that we can be. A sense of purpose for what we are doing beyond the narrow day to day existence.

Maslov's hierarchy of needs is a well known illustration of the needs that we as humans have and need to satisfy if we are to succeed and be content in our lives, and, while it is often quoted with regard to material matters, it is equally often overlooked that at the peak of his pyramid of human needs was self actualisation, in other words, to become all that we can be, but missing from most illustrations of this pyramid is the outcome of the satisfaction of these needs – the realisation, or actualisation, of the greater self above all.

Given that our individual journey through this life is personal only to ourself and no one else, how can we tap into this source of inspiration in order that it can give us the strength and fortitude to overcome all the obstacles and difficulties that life insists on throwing at us on a daily basis, in order to grow and develop, free from negativity, and with a clear intent to be all that we can be?

You will remember that earlier we spoke about losing your mind to come to your senses, well, a different way of looking at that might be to "Free your mind and open your heart". We are guided by two, often conflicting, influences, those of our head and those of our heart.

Inner Conflict.

Our head-influence is logical and draws conclusions from the knowledge that we already have and extrapolates from that knowledge, or experience, the best logical way forward. This is simply a process, a logic tree devoid of emotion; if this, then that, if that then the other, if the other then this follows and so on. If that were all there was to life then it would be pretty soulless, a simple grind, and I would not have had a job as a therapist. I would not have been needed, everything in life would have a logical explanation which all could follow to a logical conclusion and make decisions accordingly.

Thankfully, (not least for my career), there is more to life than pure logic or we would be simple robots in a soulless world. Life is far more complex, nuanced and subjective and therein arises both the problems and the opportunities for us to deal with this complex system because we also instinctively (a non-logical activity) "listen" not only to our head but also to our heart, as previously discussed.

We refer to our "heart" as the seat of instinct, intuition, interpretation and unconscious knowledge or wisdom. It is this knowledge that enables us to make leaps of logic, arriving at an answer to a situation without being able to demonstrate the logical thinking process that took us there. The fabled but much denigrated (mainly by men and wrongly so in my opinion) female intuition is perhaps the best known example of this. A woman will typically trust her instincts; a man will typically require evidence, facts or examples before arriving at a conclusion.

This is often quoted as being typical of the so-called right-sided, intuitive, artistic, "female" brain and the left sided, logical, "male" brain. It's nothing of the kind as we all use both sides of our brain and many functions are duplicated on both sides, but there is in many people a noticeably dominant preference which has arbitrarily been allocated on the lines described above. The left, logical brain tends to dominate in areas such as engineering, mathematics, physics and the right brain in the arts, music and caring professions.

Of course, this intuition is not gifted solely to the female of the species, it is just that females in general are not afraid to listen to, trust, and act upon this inner voice whereas the male of the species has blunted this innate skill through reliance upon logical thinking and distrusts such non evidence-based thinking, often to his own detriment. This intuition is the remnant of our early life as mankind when we had to rely upon our instincts, our sixth sense, for our very survival.

As a survival skill it is an offshoot of the fight or flight response mechanism that we still have embedded within us and as such is a far faster response than the slower, logical processing of our later-developed, higher-brain functions. Hence the sense of instantly "knowing" something when listening to our intuition as opposed to slowly thinking our way through to an answer.

Listen to your intuition, it is ancient knowledge breaking through the structures of the modern, developed world to bring you help and aid your survival. Carl Gustav Jung illustrated this nicely with his concept of the collective unconscious which posits that we all have access to all the knowledge of all mankind through all the ages if only we will attune ourselves to it; intuition may be one tiny example of that knowledge becoming available to us.

So, what is the point of knowing this and how can it be helpful to us on our journey of self development?

Head versus heart provides conflict and confusion in our thinking on almost any subject, almost every day. This conflict of the mind distracts and delays decision making and taking action and can lead to complete confusion and total inaction, which is rarely helpful.

It does, however, illustrate the reasons behind such confusion and the knowledge of this will help us recognise it for what it is and thereby choose to listen to, or ignore, such messages. Also, it reveals that there are aspects of our life which, while not logical and even sometimes incapable of proof, are nonetheless very real and capable of materially affecting us in everyday life.

From acting upon intuition to acting upon an unsupported belief is just one small step for mankind. Such an unsupported belief, or intuitive knowledge, might be an enormously inspirational belief that will help us transcend our own perceived limitations in pursuit of something that we believe to be for the greater good, for example, and thereby worthy of greater effort or selfless action on our journey to become all that we can be.

A belief in an unproven (or, to many, proven beyond doubt) "greater good" or spiritual entity can be inspiring, a comforting thought that life is not for nothing and that there is something more to it than the acquisition of material wealth, pleasant though that may be. There is something within mankind that craves such a comfort, that needs such a Father/Mother-on-high figure, someone to whom we can turn knowing that they will never fail us even if their wisdom and help is not immediately obvious to us, and that somehow – we are not alone.

This belief, this inspiration, can generate the positive energy that lifts our hearts and inspires positive action beyond the purely personal interests of self and this where we begin to understand the greater self, the person whom we wish to be, and what we need to do to be that person. This insight provides the energy to both inspire and drive our progress and thereby the fuller enjoyment of this life here on earth.

We have spoken about Positive Mental Attitude, the energy directed by our thoughts to create a desirable outcome. While this is a very powerful force for positive achievement in itself, it can also be enhanced by the multiplier of the belief in a greater good, a higher power, however you may wish to define that. Even without definition a blind belief will help focus our mind and direct our energies appropriately.

We are aware of our own limitations, only too well sometimes, and these tend to inhibit our attempts to achieve or progress but, of course, the greater good, by definition, has no limitations, knows no boundaries and (the clue is in the name) aims to direct our energies for the greater good which, if we align our own ambitions with this concept, will work directly in our own favour. Unlimited ability to create good in our life and good in our society, every day of our life. This is not some theoretical, goody-two-shoes approach to life but a very practical view, which is demonstrable on the ground, as we progress towards being a more complete person.

So, how do we tap into this positive energy? No doubt many of you will be relieved to hear that this has nothing to do with going to Church and singing hymns, although if that is already in your armoury of positive actions it will only add to the power of your capabilities. No, there are other, simple everyday things that we can do that will focus and direct our positive energies to create the conditions in which we can, as individuals, flourish while contributing more positively to the world around us.

Before we move on to everyday methods of enhancing our performance and hastening our progress towards our personal goal, it might be worth listening to a final message about the higher self. Positive thinking is powerful; belief in a higher self, attuned to the greater good in the world and possibly hereafter, provides a format within which it is possible to answer every question that is thrown at us, overcome every doubt about what to do next and keep us focused on the journey – namely, think of yourself as already having achieved all that you can want, you are already all that you can be, you have no further personal wants or needs and you can now dedicate yourself to being an exemplar of what you are, a demonstrator of what it is like to be a messenger of the higher force; in every given circumstance when in doubt, just ask yourself this simple question; "If I am a messenger of the higher being, the greater good, what would it/he/she want me to do in this circumstance?". Freed from personal concerns the answers often become very clear, very quickly as our conscience simply feeds the greater knowledge to us through what is now an open door of reception and trust,

If it helps by all means ask out loud, hear yourself ask the question and feel the answer arise within, trust your instinct that this is the way and make your decision. Remember from earlier examples, there are no good or bad decisions, only consequences, and if we believe the wisdom of the ancients then there is no retribution, only love and understanding. As John Lennon put it so succinctly, "All you need is love".

Few decisions are life threatening or irreversible so trust your inner voice and continue to move forward in your journey. If this all sounds a bit too spiritual for you, a bit "churchy", ask yourself what you have got to lose by giving it a try? If it works for you it can only be positive and if it doesn't work, well, you have lost nothing in trying and can turn to other methods that suit you better. Of course, it may well ignite a small flame that may grow over time until it lights up your life at a later date. Who knows? Nothing to lose.

Life is amazing, it's us that screw it up with our distrust and self limiting beliefs. Let go of the past, live now, in the moment and enjoy the rest of the journey, after all, to continue with The Beatles theme, you do have a "Ticket to Ride" all the way to the end, you might as well enjoy it.

Everyday understanding.

To be successful in meeting our aims requires not just knowledge and experience but also a particular state of mind. By this I do not mean just having a positive mental attitude but also one of focused attention, of having everything within you truly aligned towards the purpose of that which you are trying to achieve, to be above the detail of life and aware of the bigger picture, to have perspective and be aware of context; only then can we truly achieve our full potential.

Our mind is our most powerful tool, one which can push us on to achievement or hold us back in the swamp of doubt, indifference and apathy. It is vital therefore that we train our mind to be fit for purpose just as we would train our body to perform feats of strength or speed for example. Great athletes don't just turn up on the day and perform.Their peak performance is preceded by hours, days, weeks and months of training to ensure that they can perform to their very best at any given time. They call it being "in the zone", totally focused on the task in hand to the exclusion of all distractions around them.

So it is with our minds upon which we will depend for our success in our journey through life. Fortunately, the effort is not as strenuous as an athlete's preparation but it does require practise, application and some effort to get the best out of it. We too need to focus, to be there in the moment, experiencing life to the full with all of our senses, alive and alert to every opportunity for moving forward, developing and growing, enriching and always moving towards being all that we can be.

Perhaps the first consideration is to double-check with ourselves – is this the right time to begin this journey? Am I truly ready to gain new perspectives, take different lines, experience new insights and understandings, in short, is the time right and am I ready? Have I thought through my motives and understand what they mean in terms of change to my life and those who are part of my life. Should the first part of my planning merely be planning to reach the stage where I am ready, to clear the clutter from my life, get things organised in order that I can make the changes that I sense will be necessary?

There is a time to become awakened, is this the time? Am I ready?

I am ready!

Perspective.

As we have seen earlier when considering how we might eat an elephant, (one spoonful at a time), perspective is everything. What may at first sight appear to be an insurmountable problem, eating the elephant, often has both a simple solution, eating it one spoonful at a time, but may also contain hidden benefits revealed by this gaining of perspective on the problem – the perspective being that the elephant might represent many months food supply! A hidden positive from an obvious negative.

We require just such perspective when we consider our life and what we are going to do with the remainder of it, having at last arrived at the point of realisation that we can do whatever we wish to do with it – it's ours and ours alone.

At this point we are on the brink of asking, or at least considering, that great unanswerable question – what is the meaning of life? I would like to reassure the reader at this early point that I do not intend to try to answer that question; I don't know is the only answer that I have arrived at so far, so let us move on.

Although I do not know the answer to that question, and nor does anyone else probably, although they may pretend otherwise, it is one that occupies our mind as we plan for the future. How long have I got (life is famously uncertain), what am I meant to be doing with it etc etc.

Well, if we can't answer the greater question of the meaning *of* life then we can at least look at how we may find meaning *within* life because that is certainly up to us completely and is the underlaying cause, as we have discussed previously, of such phenomena as the so-called mid-life crisis as our search for meaning moves away from that which we have to that which we now feel we need.

Let me challenge you with a simple statement: Life has no meaning except that which we assign to it.

Life has no meaning! AAARGH! Does this mean that I should immediately go and throw myself off of a bridge because this life is all a big waste of time? Just before you do, consider the second half of the statement "...except that which we assign to it". People have asked me why, if I hold the complete statement to be true, I don't just do that, end my life. Well to me there seems to be a breakdown of logic in that assumption. Just because I cannot determine what the point of it all is does not mean that it does not have a point or that it isn't enjoyable, if not in whole then certainly in parts, or that I can't create meaning within it which is beneficial both to myself and to others. Isn't that a worthy aim and good enough reason for living?

For example, I assign great value to being able to help others through my work. That has meaning within this life for me and, hopefully, for my patients whose journey through their own lives may be eased somewhat by my being here. Who knows, but I believe it and that is all that matters – for me. So perspective is important.

The Buddhists would have us believe that "all life is an illusion" which at first sight appears to be a nonsensical saying; it cannot be an illusion because I am here experiencing it – aren't I?

One meaning might be that each of us creates our own illusion of what life is from looking at our life, which just "is", the world is neutral remember, and then adapting that simple experience to our own preferences based upon our prejudices, beliefs, wishes – in other words, we see what we want to see and life becomes what we want it to be rather than what it is.

If we believe that life is unfair, then life will be unfair and we will see unfairness wherever we go. If we believe that life is biased against us because of our race, colour or religion for example, then we will see that bias in everything that we see, hear and experience in the world. Another old saying neatly captures this in the phrase "If you go looking for trouble you will surely find it". Funny how all these old sayings of Granny carry so much wisdom and yet we ignore it and have to learn it all again from scratch for ourselves – or sometimes refuse to learn it because it doesn't fit our prejudiced, biased view of how the world actually is.

If we can just step back from the problem and stop shouting at the world, open our eyes and our ears to the truth, we can experience a much better place than the one that we have believed that we are living in. This is called gaining perspective.

So, life has no meaning other than that which we assign to it and all of life is an illusion anyway! Whatever next? Can this message possibly get any more weird? Well, try this for size - nothing matters.

Yes, that's right, nothing, but nothing matters – if you have perspective!

For perspective you could say "the big picture" or "the helicopter view" or "context" or any of many other phrases including one that we used earlier, the whole Gestalt, seeing things in their true context and not as isolated incidents that occur randomly to us.

Even so, *nothing* matters? That's quite a statement isn't it? Well, things only matter if we decide that they do as we said earlier, life only has the meaning that we assign to it.

Let's consider the example that we used earlier. Two lifelong friends who are sports fans go to watch a match in which both of their teams are playing each other, they sit together, watch the match together, leave together afterwards - and never speak to each other again in their life! What could possibly have happened to cause such a catastrophic rift in their friendship and their lives?

What actually happened was that a sports event took place. That's all that actually happened in the real world. Both parties observed this event, a regular weekly, ritual, commonplace event and if that were all they observed there would not be any dispute about what took part during that event and they would have discussed it amicably and moved on with their lives quite harmoniously.

But that wasn't all that they observed. Before the observing took place they both individually put on different sorts of blinkers, applied different filters, introduced various personal bigotries and values, subjective opinions and prejudices and, as a result, saw two completely different events.

For one person, a supporter of the red team, the red team were fair, honest, skilful, hard working and reaped the reward for their integrity and hard work.

For the other person, a supporter of the blue team, the red team were nothing more than a group of unprofessional, unskilled, cheating, lie-ing scoundrels who through a mixture of sheer luck and connivance, bullying and more cheating fooled the referee into making decisions that went against the blue team, who of course, were by definition, the epitome of fairness, honesty, skill, reason and integrity.

As a result of failing to agree the friends went their separate ways still wearing their blinkers with all the usual filters and prejudices in place, the poorer for losing a friend and no richer for one team having won and one team having lost.

But did it, the sporting event, matter? Did it matter more than a lifelong friendship? What changed in the world as a result of the outcome of the event?

Of course, it was only as important as the two (now ex) friends chose to make it and gave a value to it which was a greater value than they gave to their friendship. Now imagine that prior to the event you had been able to speak to them and tell them that this was how it would unfold if they didn't change their assigned values. Given this new perspective one can reasonably wonder whether, in the light of knowing what the outcome would be, whether they would not have preferred to check their assigned values of the competing team and football overall and change them to avoid the predicted outcome. Perspective can change outlook, which changes attitudes, actions and outcomes. That is why it is so important in our everyday life. Being able to step back and see the bigger picture changes the way that we relate to our own world and guides and informs our way forward to the better way of life that we seek.

Imagine what it would be like to be a leaf on a big oak tree. Imagine what you would see, thousands of other leaves like yourself doing pretty much the same as yourself, the same repetitive day in, day out process of converting sunlight to energy, boring, boring, boring and meaningless to the leaf.

Now step back from the tree and gain some perspective. Observe the majesty and beauty of this magnificent tree, dominating its' landscape, providing food and shelter for millions of insects, reinvigorating the atmosphere of the planet, an essential part of the universe. That's perspective for you. Makes one proud to be a leaf doesn't it?

Why does this gaining of perspective matter?

It matters because perspective helps us to find the middle way, a balance in life that obviates the need for entrenched opinions and tribal attitudes that lay at the root of so much trouble in the world today. If we can see both sides of an argument, the other point of view, then not only do we learn and grow as a person ourselves we also help to smooth the road for others to do the same and give others the space to find their own truth.

The message is that nothing matters so much that we need to harm or offend others, limit our life or damage the world. My opinions are just that, my opinions. Not yours and not anyone else's, and the same with yours and neither of us have the right to insist on their universal application or "rightness". Back to the black and white thinking of earlier.

We need to celebrate and respect difference by recognising that no-one, but no-one has the right answer because no-one knows what the question is. All we can do is find that which is right for ourself and try to make it fit with those around us and be ready to adapt and adjust our "truth" when we meet a greater "truth", to learn as we grow and develop. There is no one truth, only that which we choose to believe and that is itself a function of prejudice, bigotry and limited knowledge.

The more that we gain perspective on life the sooner we begin to understand that there are no arguments to win, life is not a race, it is only our own personal journey, nothing else: there are no points to score, it's not a competitive game, there is only doing the right thing. The right thing for ourself in our journey of growth and development, and, if we follow our hearts we will tap into the greater understanding and the right thing for ourself will also be the right thing for the wellbeing of the greater universe around us – how good is that?

So, are you motivated yet to do something about your life or is reading this book enough for now? Remember the old saying - I hear and I forget, I see and I remember, I do and I understand. Reading this, and other books, may prepare you for change but unless you actually do something you will soon forget the imperative to change. Once you begin with the first step and see a small change made in your life you will see what is possible. To continue with the process day by day will be to gain a greater understanding of both yourself and the world in which you live and from which will spring the ability to live within it more at peace and contentment with yourself and the others who share your world.

Chapter 9 – Journey's End.

Together we have looked at making lots of small changes in our life in order to alter our future to be something more in tune with our own self's full potential and our more informed desire. We have looked at setting goals and objectives, examined ways in which beneficial small changes may be made and for what reasons. We have undertaken a journey now towards a more fulfilling future and have touched upon the benefits, not only to ourselves of such a course of action, but also for the "greater good", however we may choose to define that for ourselves.

Whilst focusing on this journey towards our better future however, we also have to acknowledge that our own personal journey towards change and improvement is part of our even longer journey through life itself. This overall journey leads inevitably towards a conclusion that, here in the West at least, we choose to ignore until the very last moment when it is too late to make any changes other than to take out some insurance by "getting religion", and that conclusion is of course our own death in this world. As the saying has it, "Life itself is a terminal illness". However, now that we have a more considered, planned approach to our future we might like to consider how to build in some greater awareness of where we already are and where we will be until the very end of our greater journey.

No man is an island is an old saying and points out that although we are here alone, we need others to help us through life and, although this is often overlooked, others need us for the same purpose. We have spoken of the greater good and I would suggest that if we step back from the detail of our own life's interests we can see that there are others less fortunate than ourselves or even those around us who could be cheered or encouraged by our own more understanding or empathic relationship with them. There are many who we will never meet or get or know who could benefit from a less selfish world and we can be part of the change that will enhance the world around us for everyone. As we progress and change for the better let us share some of that love and happiness with others. For the cynical among you, this is similar to buying insurance early, get some points stacked up, just in case.

We touched upon the meaning of life which is too big a question for anyone to answer but we did also see that finding meaning *within* life was possible. Other lessons from the text come to mind; it is better to give than receive, allow others to help in order that they build their own self esteem and so on. So, within life we can do quite a lot to contribute to the greater good but along the way we are going to be tested, tested by ourself, by others, by life itself and we will need all the help we can get sometimes to stay positive and on track in order to be in a position to help others.

A final small point which may help in building a better future which you may wish to consider is faith. If you have a belief in the way things are, that is, that there is a purpose to everything, you may find it helpful in difficult times to think that everything that happens is exactly as it should happen for your own greater good. People who have a faith, not necessarily religious, in general tend to feel and live happier lives than those who do not, faith tends to provide a feeling of comfort and security that all will be well, that everything will work out, that, somehow, we are not alone. It is at least a comfort blanket for the here and now.

Faith is not necessarily a religious belief or practise. Many people gain extraordinary benefits from their belief in, for example, the cycle of life which is common in the East. This is the idea that we experience many lives and that death is merely the opportunity to be born again to learn new wisdom through different experience, that each life teaches us something different, all leading to a state of perfection.

It can be helpful in providing context or perspective for our troubles in this life or when facing the death of someone close knowing that they will be reborn to a better life. One question that is often asked when mourning a lost loved one is "Did you mourn your child before she was born"? Your loved one has simply gone to be reborn again. This is not death, just a passing of time, therefore there are no goodbyes. There is a tradition in Buddhism of actively going to search the world for the new Dalai Lama knowing that he/she has already been born, positive mental attitude in practise.

Death in this life is just the end of this part of the overall journey and can be seen as simply a different level of consciousness. We are familiar with our conscious world, the world that we live in and experience, but we tend not to consider the next level of consciousness which is outside of this life.

Many claim to have "second sight" or have contact with unworldly spirits, others read Tarot and appear to be able to tap into a world of knowledge that is hidden from most of us and this troubles us because we are not able to easily explain it or make sense of it. Yet children and animals also appear to have greater insight into these matters, it is just that as we grow older we lose this innocence, this sixth sense to understand these matters.

Young children gain meaning from everything that is happening around them, they are like aerials picking up signals both from the obvious world around them and from they world that they sense, unspoken conversation, the atmosphere in the room and so on. There are many, many stories of animals being aware of their owners presence long before they appear in the home or even the street they live in through apparently "sensing" their presence long before we can see them. Death in this life may be seen as an extension of that "world" that we cannot see but that we can sense at times and so, in the sense of having a positive mental attitude to carry us through such difficult times we should perhaps be looking for moments of unreasonable happiness - enjoying having the cat on our lap whilst struggling with difficult emotions, feeling good about the wind in our face whilst walking the dog during a difficult time, all these are simple reminders that life is still good, that life is to be enjoyed and that feelings of mourning are for ourselves, not the departed, a form of understandable self-pity that will pass with time; meanwhile there is still life to enjoy in simple ways.

In a way, at such times, there is a feeling that everything has changed for us but, in fact, little has changed, life goes on and we must have all our strength and composure to deal with it until the pain lessens. One lesson that I learned in such times was to be grateful for life and what it has to offer and I have developed a small habit that helps me to remember that point. At the end of every day, just before I fall into a sleeping state, I like to think of the day that has just gone by and try to think of three things that have given me pleasure, however briefly, that day and to give thanks for: spring flowers in a garden, lovely sunshine, patting a stray dog, hearing laughter; many, many small things that made the day beautiful if only for a moment and like the long journey we spoke of that is just a lot of small steps, so my day has been just a lot of small enjoyable moments.

As the oft quoted poem by an anonymous author has it:

"Do not stand at my grave and weep, for I am not there, I do not sleep.

I am a thousand winds that blow, I am the diamond glints on snow,

I am the sunlight on ripened grain, I am the gentle Autumn rain.

When you awaken in the morning's hush I am the swift uplifting rush of quiet birds in circled flight, I am the soft stars that shine at night.

Do not stand at my grave and cry, I am not there; I did not die".

During your journey through change, the old you will necessarily die to make way for the new you, so it is with life. Change is constant; welcome and endorse the many small changes that you are making already, just by reading this book you are already demonstrating your wish and desire for those changes and all that you have to do now is to make them a reality.

Chapter 10 - Postscript.

In making the many small changes that we have discussed you will have strengthened yourself in many, many, immeasurable ways such that when adversity comes again, as it will in life, you will be better prepared both mentally and emotionally, to survive the difficulty and to help others in similar circumstances at different times.

And so we come to the end of our own particular journey together, just part of the overall journey of life but an important part nonetheless, one which incorporates many small changes which, together, will lead to great change and put you on the path to becoming all that you can be, to meeting your full potential and truly living your life to the full.

You have successfully mapped out the changes that you would like to see in yourself, the next step is to implement those changes such that the wider world can see them in you as you demonstrate the new you, the you that you always knew that you could be. To keep yourself on course in living those changes imagine what you would say about yourself If you could write your own obituary of who you were, what you had achieved, what would it say? Now live that description to make it come true, enjoy the journey, hold true to yourself and your beliefs, welcome and accept the changes, revel in the new you. Enjoy your new self!

Bon Voyage.

Appendix 1 – Planning

Goal Setting

Based on the premise that if you don't know where you are going you probably won't get there this is a process to help you set short, medium and long term achievable, meaningful goals.

Step 1. Write down all the things you want to do, be, have or achieve – your Goals.

Step 2. Write in one brief sentence <u>why</u> you want to be, do, have or achieve each item on your list. If you can't do this with any of them either give them more thought or cross them off, they are not sufficiently clear in your head to be considered to be a realistic goal.

Step 3. Decide the most important areas of your life - for example...

- Family/friends (this could be 2 different areas).
- Partner/significant other person.
- Career/work.
- Financial.
- Health and vitality.
- Emotional well being.
- Social life.

- Fun and recreation.

- Physical environment (where you are living how you are living, your surroundings).

- Spiritual life.

- Add, change or delete to include all the areas of life that are important to you.

- Define what success means to you in each of the life areas you have identified.

Step 4. Take each of your goals in turn and ask the question, 'Will having, being, doing or achieving this thing improve the areas of my life that I deem are important.

Step 5. For each of your goals, ask if it is fair and reasonable to achieve this to not only yourself but everyone in your sphere of influence and concern and if it will it take you closer to your overall objective.

Step 6. Put your goals in order. Take your top "X" goals. These are the ones you are going to work on. Divide your goals into 4 main groups:-

- Ongoing goals needing daily input.

- short term goals to achieve within a week to a month.

- medium term goals that may take between a month and a year.

- long term goals that may take longer than a year.

Step 7. For each of the goals on the list expand your *"why"*. Explain to yourself fully, why you want to have this goal and what it will mean to you. Write this down.

Step 8. Take each goal in turn and make 2 *'to do'* lists for each to show:-

- what you are prepared to do to achieve it.

- what you will need to do to achieve it.

Step 9. Make a list of:-

- the people you need to work with or

- the people who can help you.

- the skills you might need to develop.

- the actions you need to take.

- what you need to learn.

- what you need to understand.

The GROW Model.

This is a basic model for change which will allow you to challenge and then formalise your intended change, putting in place firm actions agains a timescale by which you will achieve your aim. It helps to formalise your thinking from what is probably a hazy idea into a structured plan that you will have thought through and created a basic agenda to achieve that plan. GROW is an acronym for **G**oal, **R**eality, **O**ptions, **W**ay Forward, by all means adjust, adapt, change any or al of it to suit your own way of working, this is just a template, create your own best way based upon this. The only measurement is - does it work for you in helping to define and achieve your goals.

Goal.

With regard to your intended outcome or objective, take yourself forward in time to a point when it is as you would like it to be, that is, you have achieved your objective.

What do you notice that tells you that you have achieved this goal, or if it's a problem, how do you know that you have solved it?

1. What are you **doing** that shows that you have achieved this?

2. What are you **hearing** that tells you that you have achieved your goal?

3. How are you **feeling** at this point in the future?

4. What are you **saying**, to yourself or others?

5. When do you want to be in this position that you can see in the future? What timescale do you have in mind? Next month, next year? Be realistic. If it's a big career goal, break it down to parts that we can focus on in a shorter timescale.

6. How challenging or exciting is this goal for you? If it seems to be too challenging, break it down to be achievable within the timescale set at 5 above, or amend 5 to be realistic. If it is not challenging enough you will get bored and give up – do we need to make it more challenging? In what way, reduce timescale for example?

7. How will you know that you have achieved your goal, is there a specific measurement that we can apply?

8. Where do you have control or influence with regard to this goal, people, money, circumstance, location etc...

9. Where do you NOT have influence or control with regard to this goal?

10. Is there anyone else that we need to be aware of with regard to your goal.

11. How will the achievement of your goal affect those around you, family, partner, friends, work colleagues etc? Will they help or obstruct you?

REALITY.

1. What is it about this issue or problem that makes it an issue or problem for you right now?

2. As well as what is happening, what is missing from your current situation that you would like to have present?

3. What is happening/present in your life that you would like to keep happening/present to contribute to achieving your goal?

4. What have you done so far to improve matters or start on achieving your goal?

5. What were the results of these actions?

6. What obstacles or barriers are there in your way that might prevent or hinder you in moving forward?

7. What resources do you have to help you to achieve your desired goal? (skills, experience, qualifications, personal qualities, talents, time, enthusiasm, money, support, contacts etc).

8. What other resources will you need?

9. Where can you get them from? Who has them? Identify requirements.

10. Finally, look back at your stated goal, is it still accurate and relevant, or has it changed? Make any changes and review all that follows in the new definition.

OPTIONS.

(Brainstorm, fantasise, keep free from judgement, criticism or limiting thoughts, write it all down, omit nothing no matter how unlikely.)

1. What COULD you do to move yourself just one step forward RIGHT NOW?

2. What else could you do if you didn't have to explain what you were doing or be answerable to anyone else?

3. What could you do if money wasn't an issue – unlimited?

4. If you could devote all of your time to this one thing, what would you do then?

5. What COULD you do if you didn't have to live with the consequences?

6. If you went to a more knowledgable person what might they suggest?

7. If you went to a friend what might they suggest?

8. If you went to your partner what might they suggest?

9. If, deep down, you secretly knew what you should do first, what would it be?

10. Think back over your list, do any of those answers suggest any new idea for you.

11. Choose one of the options – one that will move you forward just one step. Choose the easiest thing to do, or the cheapest, or the quickest, or the one that you feel most comfortable doing, but choose one RIGHT NOW! Highlight it.

12. Think about your goal, will this take you on the first step to achieving that goal?

13. What is the benefit of doing this one thing? Will it make you feel better? Will it mean that you know something new? Will it relieve some stress? There has to be a benefit? Identify it and write it down.

14. Will choosing this one thing really help you achieve your goal?

15. How will you feel when you have achieved this first step?
    How will others think about you for having done it?

THE WAY FORWARD.

1. What are you going to do? BY WHEN?

2. What must you do to complete this action that you have
    chosen?

3. When are you going to begin taking these actions? What is
    your timescale?

4. How long do you think that this list of actions will take you?
    Identify anticipated time scales for each item?

5. Should anyone else be involved in this list of questions
    you're going to do to complete this thing, issue or goal that
    you have chosen?

6. What do you want/need this person/people to do??

7. When will you tell them?

8. Who else should know that you are doing these things?

9. When will you tell them if not now?

10. Is there anyone who should NOT know that you are doing
    these things? WHY? How does that conflict/agree with your
    own value/belief systems?

11. Whatever your first step is, can you think of any obstacle or
    barrier that might stop you from doing it? WHY?

12. How likely is it to stop you? Is it more likely or not likely to stop you?

13. If more likely, what can you do to make your first step more achievable? (This then becomes the first step)

14. How will you overcome this obstacle?

15. What will stop you from doing it?

16. Earlier you wrote down the time by when you would complete this first step. Is this time still valid?

17. Is there anything else that you need to consider before you begin this first step like finance, parents, partners – anything at all?

18. You have identified when you want to achieve your goal and roughly when you will begin. When **precisely** will you now start. **SPECIFICALLY** – day, date, time, place. **WRITE IT IN YOUR DIARY. Finally, on scale of 1-10, how likely is it that you will do it? You are on your way! Congratulations!**

Appendix 2 - CBT Procedure.

This simple process is designed to help you analyse just why you think, do and say the things that you do and to illustrate a more acceptable alternative. This is based on the notion that there is a circular link between what we <u>think</u>, how we are made to <u>feel</u> by those thoughts and how those feelings directly affect our <u>actions</u>. Change any one and the other two change in consequence.

A.

1. Identify a troublesome thought. (For example, this person doesn't like me)

2. Write out a list of unhelpful <u>feelings</u> that this generates. (For example, I feel inadequate, immature, embarrassed, aggressive etc)

3. Note how you <u>react</u> to these thoughts e.g. blushing, stammering, aggression, arguing).

B.

Now create a separate list which directly contradicts the points in 2. above, that is, positive affirmations. (For example, I feel confident, I am OK, they can't hurt me, they are themselves probably feeling insecure).

C.

Note how your feelings have changed as a result of your positive thinking and how you feel able to behave differently I.e. less aggressively, less passively, more confidently.

The point of this is to demonstrate to ourselves that there are always two views on anything and that although we may have taken a negative view of something which leads to negative behaviour we can also flip the coin and see the other side. This gives us a more balanced view of anything and alleviates some of the negativity that we experience when our thinking is isolated within ourselves. The simple act of writing it down frees up the alternatives for us to experience.

APPENDIX 3 - Epithets and Out-takes.

Many of the points made within this text may be easily summarised in short, pithy statements which may, in turn, act as a short cut when re-visiting this text; so here are a few of the main points in summary:

We are where we are (not necessarily where we would choose to be).

It is what it is, deal with it.

Life is not fair, accept it.

To be happy/unhappy is a choice.

Lose your mind and come to your senses. (Stop thinking, start feeling)

If you keep doing what you have always done, you will keep getting the result you have always got.

Choose to change.

It's your life, no one else's.

If you don't know where you are going how will you know when you get there?

This is the way it is – at the moment. It will change.

Start creating memories today.

Live in, and enjoy, the moment.

If you waste this moment either regretting the past or fearing the future you lose this moment and it won't come back.

Tomorrow is promised to no-one.

Stop "what-iff"ing, start doing.

Put on your oxygen mask, people need you.

Only you are responsible for your life.

Change is natural, stop resisting and enjoy.

We can't control life, we can only influence it.

Musts, should's, oughts are stress creators, ignore them.

We only learn from our failures.

I intend to keep failing until I succeed.

Manage expectations.

Eat Elephants one spoonful at a time.

The longest journey is made up of lots of small steps.

Whether you think you can or you think you can't, you are probably right.

Be the change that you want to see in the world.

Positive Mental Attitude = psychosomatic wellness.

Blow into your own sails, no one else will.

The difference between a dream and a plan is a time limit.

Step out of your own shadow.

80/20 rule.

There are no good or bad decisions, only consequences.

Become all that you can be.

Life is your own journey, not a competition with anyone else.

Think of three things that made you (even briefly) happy today.

Small changes make big differences.

Seek unreasonable happiness in difficult situations.

Life is a terminal illness, enjoy it while you have it.

Happiness is contagious, go contaminate as many as you can.

Printed in Great Britain
by Amazon

43620578R00071